COMPOSING OLANA

COMPOSING OLANA

A JOURNEY ON FOOT THROUGH FREDERIC CHURCH'S GREATEST WORK OF ART

Annik LaFarge

EMPIRE STATE EDITIONS
AN IMPRINT OF FORDHAM UNIVERSITY PRESS
NEW YORK 2026

Funding for this book was provided by

Furthermore: a program of the J. M. Kaplan Fund.

Map by Marty Schnure.

Fordham University Press also publishes its books in a variety of electronic formats. Some content that appears in print may not be available in electronic books.

Visit us online at www.fordhampress.com/empire-state-editions.

For EU safety / GPSR concerns: Mare Nostrum Group B.V., Mauritskade 21D, 1091 GC Amsterdam, The Netherlands, gpsr@mare-nostrum.co.uk

Library of Congress Cataloging-in-Publication Data available online at https://catalog.loc.gov.

Printed in the United States of America

28 27 26   5 4 3 2 1

First edition

Dedicated in memory, love, and gratitude to my teachers,
from my earliest days to today:

Eleonor Bindman, Rafael Cortés, Judith Conant, Kitty Cunningham,
Rick Darke, Mary de Kay, Kelleher Jewett, Susan Knox, Don Gifford,
Thomas Mallon, Jean Fair Mitchell, Kathy Watson Neilsen,
Claude de France Smith, Betsy Sylvester, Frances Taliaferro,
Delight Tolles, E. K. Weedin Jr., Barbara Winslow

CONTENTS

AUTHOR'S NOTE

This is a book about an American landscape, set in New York's Hudson River Valley.

Those are words—*American, landscape, Hudson River*—that I use throughout the text, and I do so with an awareness that they reflect an evolving understanding of the peoples and cultures that have called this area home for at least ten thousand years. The Indigenous peoples who were here before European settlers arrived in the early seventeenth century, chiefly the Mohicans, who called themselves Muh-he-con-ne-ok, or People of the Waters That Are Never Still, had many names for the river we now call the Hudson. The continent where they lived, hunted, fished, and farmed was not known to them as "America." In recent years their place in this story has been brought to light by new scholarship and a deepening appreciation for the meaning of the word "land" in landscape.

One of the joys of researching this book was discovering so much of the history that lives in this valley. In the pages that follow I have done my best to make legible, wherever possible, the presence and stories of the people who lived in, and revered, what we today call the Hudson River Valley, long before it became famous for the painters who launched this country's first homegrown, or native, art movement, which came to be known as the Hudson River School. That includes a great many female artists whose extraordinary contributions to American landscape painting have been ignored, and therefore left unknown, for far too long.

Those of us who live in and visit this corner of the United States are exceedingly lucky to have Olana and the Thomas Cole Site within easy walking distance of each other. Season after season the people who work in these national historic sites—curators of art and landscape, docents, archivists, graduate students, administrators, volunteers—put together exhibits, catalogs, books, films, webinars, and lectures that shine new light on the highly diverse, rich history of this place.

Of all the many reasons cultural institutions like these are important, perhaps the greatest is their capacity to surprise. I hope the reader of *Composing Olana* will share that joy of discovery in the pages ahead. If you find yourself hungry to learn more, you will be richly rewarded by a visit to the bookstores at both sites, and you can further support their work by becoming a member at Olana.org and ThomasCole.org.

COMPANION WEBSITE

Because *Composing Olana* was designed for black-and-white images only, I created a companion website that mirrors the book's organization and provides hundreds of photos: of the carriage roads at Olana in every season of the year; the magnificent—and magnificently colorful—house at the top of the hill that Frederic Edwin Church built for his family; features of the landscape that inspired Church and his teacher, Thomas Cole, such as the strikingly beautiful and sometimes architectural dead trees that fill the forest; works from the many outdoor public art exhibitions at Olana over the years; multiple views of the "Bend in the River" that was, and remains, a centerpiece of Olana's viewshed; landmarks in the Catskill Mountains; vestiges of the last ice age that appear throughout the landscape; paintings and sketches by some of the artists who are important to this story; links to recordings of music and other features in the Olana soundscape; and much, much more.

Each of the eight sections on the website corresponds to the related section of the book and includes page numbers for handy reference. If you don't see a picture in this book, you'll likely find it—and a few alternate views—on the website, OlanaBook.com.

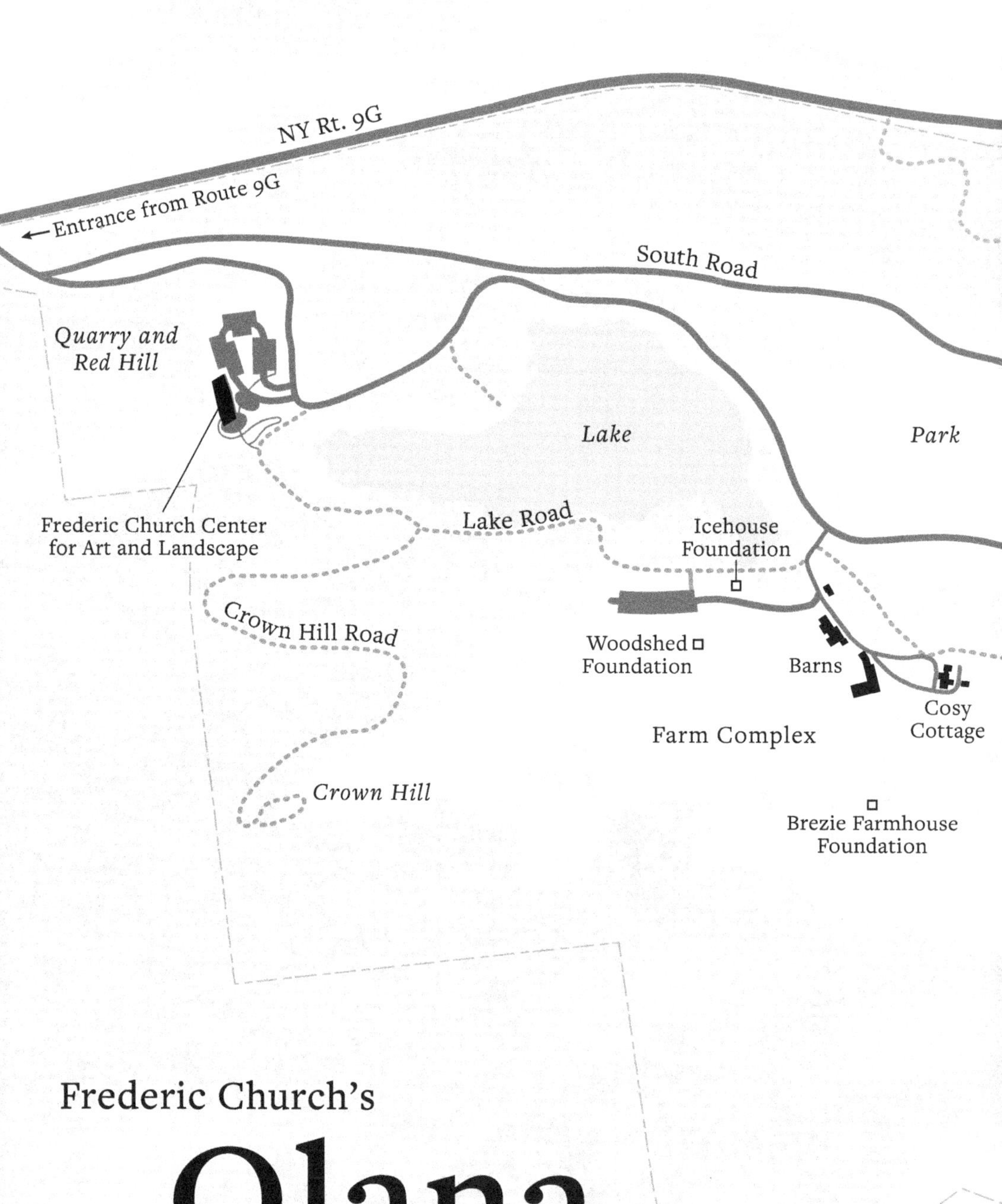

Frederic Church's Olana

A Rambler's Map

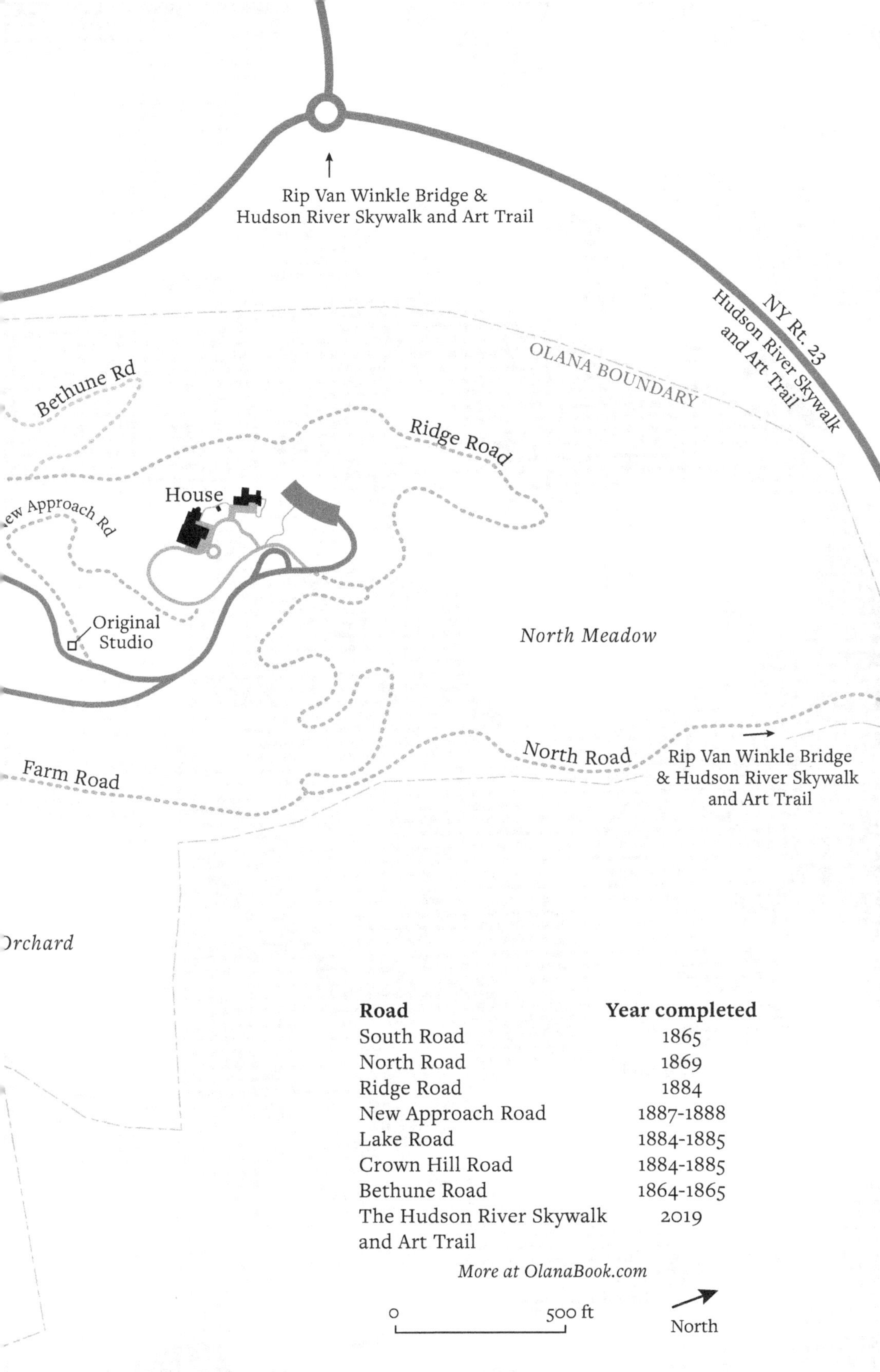

Road	Year completed
South Road	1865
North Road	1869
Ridge Road	1884
New Approach Road	1887-1888
Lake Road	1884-1885
Crown Hill Road	1884-1885
Bethune Road	1864-1865
The Hudson River Skywalk and Art Trail	2019

COMPOSING OLANA

Olana in winter, from the frozen lake.

INTRODUCTION

Every landscape tells a story.

I began this work of excavating the history of my own place in words and pictures after moving to a loft in West Chelsea where, just outside my window, the High Line park was being completed. Researching *On the High Line* was an act of urban exploration and discovery. The old viaduct roughly follows the original coastline along the west side of Manhattan, running over land that was once home to the Lenape people and centuries later became a central artery in New York's Industrial Revolution. In 1934, when it was completed, Robert Moses's High Line was greeted as an ingenious transportation innovation: an elevated freight railroad that ran parallel to the Hudson River and snaked through buildings and warehouses like a massive conveyor belt above the congested city streets. As I tuned myself into this landscape, everywhere I looked I found a story. Indeed, along this one sliver of land that stretches from Gansevoort to Thirty-Fourth Street you can find virtually every element of the New York saga. Shortly, I stopped seeing the famous grid of Manhattan and saw instead layers of landscape which, taken together, convey the rich history of our little "island at the center of the world." *On the High Line* ended up being more than just a book about New York's most popular new park; it was about how to read a landscape and the joys of uncovering stories about place that help us understand where we came from and who we have become.

I was in my mid-twenties when I bought my first house in the Hudson Valley, a small Civil War–era saltbox about four miles from another of New York's most original and beloved parks, the home and landscape of Frederic Edwin Church known as Olana. Most people who know about Frederic Church know him as a painter, and fresh out of college that was true for me. It would be many years before I came to understand the full meaning of this place and the true size of this extraordinary artist's canvas.

If you can imagine yourself sitting in a small wooden cart, gazing through the ears of a snow-white donkey as you're pulled along winding roads through

W. E. R. LaFarge and Annik LaFarge, June 1987.

one of our country's most magnificent and storied landscapes, you'll have an idea of how Frederic Church wanted you to experience Olana. There are no longer donkeys here, and today the docents and staff use electric, open-sided vehicles to escort visitors through the park, but the carriage roads and views are intact, and together they tell a great American story.

This book was designed to deepen the experience of Olana by making legible everything one sees in its landscape, as well as so much that remains invisible: a momentous seventeenth century Indian battle that took place on a little island in view from Ridge Road, for example, and the grand, Greek Revival hotel that once perched on a rock ledge in the Catskills and ushered in the first wave of Hudson Valley tourism in the early years of the nineteenth century. *Composing Olana* brings the story up to date, but it also looks backward hundreds and even thousands of years to present the characters and events that constitute a lesser-known preface.

• • •

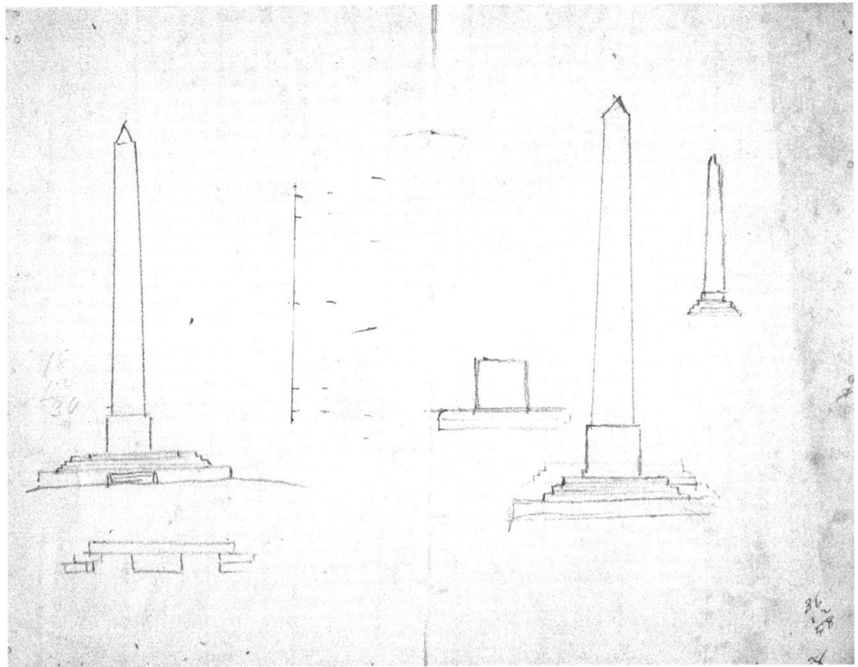

Frederic Edwin Church, *Designs for the Podium of Cleopatra's Needle, New York* (verso), c. 1879–1880, graphite on paper, 7 7/8 × 10.

Frederic Church was the most famous and financially successful American painter of his generation, and his influence as a placemaker continues to be felt by millions of people, from Central Park to Niagara Falls. Frederick Law Olmsted and Calvert Vaux are universally credited with the design of New York's first great park, but less well known is that they highly valued the contribution Frederic Church made to its design—the "art element," as Olmsted referred to it in an 1871 letter. "We were anxious," he wrote, "that the public utility of devotion to art & the study of nature in a public service of this kind should be recognized and Church seemed on the whole the most appropriate and respectable man to express this." Here is another little-known fact to consider next time you're in Central Park and pass the marvelous Egyptian obelisk known as Cleopatra's Needle that stands behind the Metropolitan Museum of Art: You can thank Frederic Church for both its placement and the base of the sculpture, which he helped design.

Olmsted also credited Church for sparking the campaign to save Niagara

Falls, for it was he who first sounded the alarm about encroaching development, tourism, and the "rapidly approaching ruin of its characteristic scenery." Here too is a place where Church's name doesn't resonate as it should. Historian John K. Howat concluded that "the restoration and salvation of Niagara Falls as a scenic marvel can properly be attributed to him," thanks to his paintings of the Falls, which helped raise the site "to the status of international icon." In addition to his role as a commissioner of the New York City Department of Parks, Church was a cofounder and trustee of the Met. One of the great adventurers of the nineteenth century, he was also a founder of The Travellers, a society of distinguished gentlemen, limited to twenty-five individuals, who sought to understand and explain the world through the pursuit of science, music, literature, and art.

Most people who know about his work and life think of Church's home in the Hudson Valley as a Persian-inspired castle on a hill, but over the past decade the emphasis at Olana, today a National Historic Landmark, has shifted from the house to the naturalistic landscape Church created here. What is surprising in this story is that toward the end of his life Church believed this landscape to be his greatest work of art. In the 1870s, suffering from severe rheumatoid arthritis, he turned his artist's eye to the 250 acres he owned on a prominent elevation overlooking the Hudson River and began crafting a space of wonder and beauty for the benefit of family, friends, and visitors. Having built his artistic career on the immersive, touring panoramas that were all the rage in nineteenth-century America—works like *Heart of the Andes*, *Cotopaxi*, *The Icebergs*, *Niagara*, and *Rainy Season in the Tropics*—he now treated the landscape itself as a canvas. "I have made about 1 3/4 miles of road this season," he wrote in an 1884 letter, "opening entirely new and beautiful views." He used the physical landscape to create a series of events: woodland, meadow, lake, orchard, terraced lawn, wetland, park. *Foreground, middle ground, background.* Where once he had applied these elements to the canvas in his studio, Church now worked in the landscape itself, a 360-degree, three-dimensional space that could convey everything a painting could and perhaps even more. Decades into his project he wrote to a friend, "I can make more and better landscapes in this way than by tampering with canvas and paint in the studio."

• • •

The story of Olana begins in 1844 when a young Frederic Church came to the Hudson Valley to study with Thomas Cole, then considered one of America's most innovative landscape painters. Church's father was a prosperous, respected businessman in Hartford, Connecticut, and a supporter and friend of Daniel Wadsworth, founder of the Atheneum. In his museum Wadsworth had several paintings by Thomas Cole, and they were old friends. In a letter to Cole in May 1844 Wadsworth asked the great painter if he would take on a young, talented, artist who was hungry for mentorship and learning. And there was more: Could Frederic come and live with the Cole family? Cole answered *yes* to both, and Church became his first student. (History records only one other student in Cole's lifetime: Benjamin McConkey, a young artist from Cincinnati, Ohio, who came to Catskill to study with the famous painter in 1845.)

In the two years that Church spent studying with Cole, Thomas took his young student into the mountains and shared his deep, almost religious, rev-

(left) Frederic Edwin Church. Courtesy Century Association Archives. (right) Thomas Cole, ca. 1845, in a portrait by Mathew Brady. National Portrait Gallery, Smithsonian Institution.

erence for nature. He also instructed Church in the art and practice of observation, teaching the young painter to annotate his sketches with handwritten notes about everything he perceived: the colors in the sky, the shape of the clouds, the texture of leaves, the details of plants and trees. Later he would take his sketches into the studio and produce glorious, fully realized, oil paintings of the landscapes he had tramped through with his teacher. As time went by he applied this practice in his travels around New England and the American South, and eventually around the globe: to Labrador to paint icebergs; to South America, Jamaica, Europe, and the Middle East.

It's hard to imagine it today, when we're confronted with photographs everywhere we turn, but when Thomas Cole took up his paintbrush in the 1820s pictorial images of the American landscape were exceedingly rare, and citizens of this young country had no idea what lay beyond their own forests and fields. If our ancestors knew by the early 1800s what it meant to be American in political and human terms, it was the artists of the Hudson River School who showed them what it meant to be an American in *situational* terms: They connected the American spirit to the American place. In an era before the widespread availability of photographs and tourism, the Hudson River School painters conjured the unique physical qualities and stunning natural beauty of a country long considered inferior to the storied lakes, mountains, and skies of Europe.

The Hudson River School painters were also pioneering in the subjects they chose. In the early years of the nineteenth century the traditional English philosophy of painting still had its hold on American artists. As art historian Barbara Babcock Millhouse writes in her seminal book *American Wilderness: The Story of the Hudson River School of Painting*, in the eighteenth century "the status of an artist was determined by the kind of subject he chose to paint," and historical, biblical and allegorical subjects "held the highest rank" because they depicted heroism and what were considered "universal truths that contributed to the moral improvement of mankind." In the first decades of the nineteenth century when Thomas Cole, who is universally considered the father the Hudson River School, applied his brush to the subject of the American landscape itself, it was a major departure from tradition. His friend and fellow artist Asher Durand articulated the new philosophy of the American Romantic painters when he wrote that the goal of the artist was to reveal "the deep meaning of the real creation around and within us."

Within fifteen years of his arrival in Catskill, Frederic Church had become the most famous and financially successful artist in America. In 1863 a New York newspaper enthused that "a new painting by Mr. Church is as considerable an event in the world of art as a new novel by Victor Hugo, or a new poem by Tennyson, would be in the literary world." In 1860, after receiving a record $10,000 from the sale of *Heart of the Andes*, Church invested the entire amount in a parcel of land in New York's Columbia County, just a few miles south of the city of Hudson, and began working on the design of Olana. Over the next thirty years he acquired a total of 250 acres, built five miles of carriage roads, and escorted visitors in carts drawn by exotic white donkeys he had imported from Syria, up and around winding paths that were paved with crushed red stone from his own quarry. Church's tours were a dramatic, almost cinematic, way to bring visitors to a variety of composed views as they emerged around bends in the road. The scenery changes constantly: forest, river, mountains, garden, lake, interrupted every now and again with startling views of the majestic, fortress-like villa at the top of the hill, of its porches, cornices, multicolored stone walls, and a minaret that peeks up through the trees.

Today historians consider Olana to be the best-preserved historic artist's environment in America, one of the few in which the studio, house, and landscape remain essentially as the artist created them. David Huntington, an art history professor at Smith College who led the charge to save Olana from being sold and falling into private hands in the 1960s, described its place in the American story in an interview for an oral history project. "There's something of the archetypal about it," he said, observing that "so much of American culture has been distilled" in tangible, visible, form, in this place. He was a "Yankee of Yankees . . . one of our most profoundly American artists." Huntington was the first of many historians to compare Olana to two other monuments of national art and culture, the palace at Versailles and Thomas Jefferson's home at Monticello. But one of the striking things about the house at Olana is its international style, both in the architecture and the extraordinary collection of items Church and his wife Isabel brought home from their travels around the globe. "I see Olana as a one-man world's fair," Huntington said, referring to the extravagant, marvelous diversity of stuff the Churches brought home from their travels around the world: elements of Hindu, Chinese, Japanese, Mexican, Persian, and Central American art and culture.

But my main focus in this book will remain on the landscape, and this too has been astonishingly well preserved. A report made in 2002 noted how few "intrusions" there have been on the viewshed, and this gets to another major theme in the Olana story: preservation and conservation. Two major battles were engaged by local activists and the leadership at Olana in the twentieth century, one to stop a nuclear power plant in the western part of the viewshed and another to prevent the largest coal-fired cement plant in North America from being built in the eastern part. Both stories have a happy ending, the most remarkable of which was the decision in the first battle, when a painting by Frederic Church that had been placed into evidence during hearings in Albany became the powerful juggernaut that stopped a nuclear power plant.

The Olana Partnership, the nonprofit partner with the New York State Office of Parks, Recreation, and Historic Preservation (NYS Parks) that manages the property and collections, continues to lobby for the safeguarding of its viewshed, and as of 2025 nearly three thousand acres of land have been strategically protected—a cause the artist himself would robustly applaud. I know this because in the archive of correspondence at Olana is an extraordinary letter from an executive at the American Telephone and Telegraph Co. apologizing to Church—"I regret exceedingly," he begins—that the new communication lines the company was laying out in the west-facing part of the landscape had caused the painter "so much annoyance." Edward P. Meany assured Church that his foreman would not "leave your neighborhood until he had fully satisfied you in every particular." If you, like me, can't imagine that kind of thing happening at AT&T today, you're beginning to get a sense of the magic of this place and this artist.

And Church himself is beginning to be seen as an early voice in the field of conservation. One of the most fascinating sources I encountered in my research was a thesis about Church's contribution to wilderness preservation written in 1995 by Beverly Astrachan, a student of the eminent Church historian Barbara Novak. Having studied Church's plans and correspondence, Astrachan considers his project of simultaneously planting thousands of native trees and establishing a parkland as an "attempt to harmonize the opposing forces of nature and culture." She argues that "in laying out his landscape garden, Church was motivated not only by artistic concerns, but by practical, humanitarian, and ecological concerns as well." His ultimate concern, Astrachan says, is "in allowing nature to regain a central position in areas where it had previously been wiped out"—an ecological catastrophe Church would have been familiar with from his reading of a landmark book by George Perkins Marsh, an American diplomat cited by Bill McKibben as "the first modern environmentalist."

Published in 1864, Marsh's book *Man and Nature* sounded a warning about the demise of the American landscape and, after years of logging and deforestation, argued that Americans had a moral obligation to plant trees. It was an early, perhaps the first, call in this country for a radical rethinking about the human hand in the natural world, acknowledging that mankind can, and indeed had, altered the physical condition of the earth and that "the harmonies of nature" are "never broken with impunity." Informed by both his own observations and the most current ecological science of the day, Marsh decried "the ravages committed by man" and warned that Nature "avenges herself upon the intruder by letting loose upon her defaced provinces destructive energies." He believed that "self-preservation requires us to restore the equilibrium," but doing so could only happen with "great political and moral revolutions." Church experienced something of a revolution within himself in his later years. "I like wood for architectural purposes less and less as I grow older," he wrote to his friend, the sculptor Erastus Dow Palmer, in 1884. "Wood is awfully convenient and cheap just now but I suppose when our forests are swept away by the axe and fire we will use more stone and tiles instead of shingles" for our homes.

While the words "conservationist" and "preservationist" were not used in Church's time as they are today, it is now possible, reading Beverly Astrachan's closely argued essay, to see him as a kind of precursor to the work that would be done more than a century later by a great many people, beginning with

David Huntington's campaign in the 1960s, who have worked to protect Olana and, in later years, its viewshed. Her suggestion that the larger garden at Olana can be seen as "a reflection of Church's awareness of and personal contribution to the nascent wilderness preservation movement" resonates powerfully with a modern visitor.

• • •

This book is, above all else, a paean to the art of observation. Like his fellow Romantics, Frederic Church was preoccupied with the practice of observation and measurement, and was greatly influenced by naturalist Alexander Von Humboldt, who undertook an unprecedented, holistic study of the scientific processes—in botany, geology, meteorology, hydrology, geography, climatology, chemistry—that shape the natural environment, arguing that the forces of nature throughout the regions of the world are connected and interrelated. Humboldt believed that a "profound appreciation of nature . . . leads us into another and higher sphere of ideas," and that it was artists—and specifically landscape painters—who could most faithfully open this imaginative door to the masses. Church, inspired by this humanizing call to undertake scientific observation in the service of art, traveled in Humboldt's footsteps across South America, and throughout his remarkable career he imbued his paintings with both realism and poetry. His large-scale works toured the country, and they drew huge crowds. For the 1857 *Niagara* he used an unconventional format—the painting is twice as wide as it is high—to convey a panoramic expanse, and the effect was thrilling. In one city after another people lined up to pay an admission fee of twenty-five cents to immerse themselves in this as-yet unknown corner of their country.

Church would have encountered, in the first dozen pages of George Perkins Marsh's book, ideas that echoed the guidance of his teacher, Thomas Cole. Marsh writes that his intention with *Man and Nature* was "to stimulate, not to satisfy curiosity," and to coach readers into becoming closer and better observers of what was happening in the natural world. For Marsh, "the study of nature" was akin to a moral obligation, but it was not something that could be taught. "Self is the schoolmaster whose lessons are best worth his wages," he wrote, and whether you were a natural philosopher, poet, painter, sculptor, or simply a "common observer," you had no better pedagogue than yourself. "Sight is a faculty," he acknowledged, "seeing, an art." It was a credo Church carried with him throughout his life and work as both landscape architect and painter. His correspondence is filled with the joys of observation. He reveled in the constant changes wrought on the landscape by weather, light, climate, temperature, position of the sun, river tides—forces that Humboldt so faithfully observed and quantified. "We are having splendid Meteoric displays," Church wrote to a friend in 1870, "Magnificent sunsets and Auroras—red, green, yellow, and blue." They were so distracting he was "drawn away from my usual steady devotion to the new house to sketch some of the fine things hung in the sky."

I would like to now sketch for you some of the fine things in this beautiful, singular, place known as Olana. The pages ahead do not constitute a traditional, linear narrative; like my High Line book, this one is more jazz improvisation than classical sonata, to use a musical metaphor. I've organized the text around the seven main carriage roads at Olana—South Road, North Road, Ridge Road, New Approach Road, Lake Road, Crown Hill Road, Bethune Road—and the Hudson River Skywalk and Art Trail that connects Olana with the Thomas Cole Historic Site. The entries in each section unpack everything a visitor sees, occasionally hears, and often *doesn't* see in the landscape, whether that is a historical event or figure, a theme, cultural trend, or something that, like a magnet, attracted my obsessive nature and wouldn't let go, like the buckthorn fence I tramped all over Olana in search of discovering. (And, happily, did.) *Composing Olana* is designed to complement the experience of being here, and of passing through, this remarkable place. It's worth noting that readers looking for a deeper dive into the life and art of Frederic Church finally have the chance to read a full, narrative, biography, thanks to Victoria Johnson's *Glorious Country: How Frederic Church Brought the World to America and America to the World,* which was published on the two hundredth anniversary of the artist's birth in 2026.

Hovering over so much of my text, and this place, is the ghost of Frederic

Edwin Church, a man whose company I came to greatly enjoy, even treasure, on my almost daily walks at Olana. Glimpses of his character—his marvelous humor, reverence for nature and science, profound gifts of observation and hunger for knowledge about the world—infuse these pages. Walking through Olana, I am sometimes reminded of what happened during the premiere of Ludwig Von Beethoven's Ninth Symphony, the one with the stirring choral movement set to the poem "An die Freude" (Ode to Joy), that took place in 1824, just two years before Church's birth. Beethoven, by then totally deaf, conducted the orchestra himself, and when the piece came to its end the composer, who was several bars behind, continued waving his arms at the musicians. A contralto in the chorus approached Beethoven and gently turned him around so he could see, since he couldn't hear, the ecstatic applause of the audience. By the 1870s, when he was in his fifties, Church began to suffer from the extreme pain of rheumatoid arthritis, and within a decade the disease had progressed to the point where he was severely disabled. A reporter for the *Christian Intelligencer*, F. N. Zabriskie, took a tour of Olana in September 1884 and noted, at the end of his article, how it gave him "a feeling of sadness to pass the deserted [studio] building" where Church had worked on so many of his most famous paintings, before "he was obliged to lay down his brush, perhaps forever." But Zabriskie wasn't entirely correct when he told his readers that the artist's "health is so broken that life has become chiefly a struggle against disease," because in October of that year Church reported he had completed almost a mile of road building that season, including work on the pleasure drive he called Ridge Road. The following year he began working on Crown Hill Road. Frederic Church's response to his malady, to reinvent himself as an artist of landscape, is why we have this glorious public park and beautifully preserved house.

This is the story of that work of art.

Christmas Eve sled ride, 2021.

Frederic Church's composed view of the house, reflected in the lake, and the long meadow known as the Park.

SECTION 1: SOUTH ROAD, 1865

Unless you come by foot via the Hudson River Skywalk, chances are you'll arrive at Olana in a car, and as you enter the property you'll pass what looks like a secret, forested, chamber at your right. There is a sheer cliff with trees growing, almost defiantly, out of the rock face, which has a distinctly reddish tint. This is Red Hill, Frederic Church's quarry. It is closed to visitors, and you'll miss it if you're not paying close attention. Entering Olana is the perfect time to introduce readers to the ice age geology that shaped the landscape so beloved of the Hudson River School painters, and this quarry is our first teacher. The high, shale bluff of Red Hill also happens to be the first area of his future home that Church ever visited, when he tramped up the hill with his teacher, Thomas Cole, in May 1845, to sketch the magnificent views of the Catskills across the river.

Robert Titus, a geologist who, with his wife Johanna, has spent many decades analyzing and interpreting the region's deep past, explains that most of

The quarry at Red Hill.

the landscape at Olana is made of "bedded chert," better known as flint. It developed from tiny, single-celled organisms called radiolarians that inhabited the deep, dark, cold marine trench that existed here hundreds of millions of years ago. After they died the shells of these creatures accumulated on the bottom of the sea and over time their exoskeletons hardened into bedded chert. Titus speculates that "the old ocean must have produced enormous, truly astronomical, numbers of these creatures because they have produced hundreds of feet of bedded chert."

This stone was too brittle to support the magnificent house Church would build at the top of what the Dutch had named Sienghenburgh, or Long Hill, in the 1870s, but in the quarry at Red Hill he was able to harvest a fine-grained sandstone you'll see on the façade: a relic of the ice age that became part of the artist's palette when he worked as architect of his own home. It was also the crushed stone he used on his carriage roads, which in some places is still visible beneath a visitor's feet. One fine example is the little triangle where Ridge and North Roads meet at the top of what is today called Church Hill. This natural color became a kind of signature at Olana; in 1871 a newspaper article recounted how Church's "beautiful wife" could be seen "riding across those red-veined hilltops upon a milk-white donkey . . . with her baby slung in a panier." When The Olana Partnership restored the carriage roads, it imported a sandstone from Pennsylvania that was similar in color to the Red Hill stone and capable of sustaining vehicular traffic, and this is what we see beneath our feet today.

In their book *The Hudson River Schools of Art and Their Ice Age Origins*, the Tituses make a compelling argument that it was the last ice age that created the Hudson River School, and on summer walking tours Robert sports a T-shirt that says "No Glaciers, No Paintings." In other words: The vast body of work that scholars consider to be America's first native art culture would not exist without the Laurentide ice sheet, which descended on the Hudson Valley some twenty thousand years ago and, over time, sculpted the landscape into what we see today: the Catskill Mountains to the west; the Berkshires, Greens, and Taconics to the east; and the Hudson River, cutting a path from the Adirondacks to New York City. These are all elements that Frederic Church, as he crafted his miles of carriage roads, intended for us to see, and throughout the

An especially fine erratic in the picnic area at Ridge Road.

different walks we will encounter artifacts of the ice age, from the steep, almost clifflike hills around Ridge, North, and Bethune Roads to large, shapely, boulders that are scattered about the landscape and are known to geologists as "erratics."

Another important feature of South Road is the uneven line it traces as it brings visitors into the world of Olana. Church designed it at an angle to the public road below (today's Route 9G), which landscape architect Robert Toole, who wrote the foundational historic landscape report for Olana, explains was a newly popular device in the nineteenth century that could take travelers through "a kaleidoscope of visual situations." The bending, winding entrance road is a foretaste of what is to come in the carriage roads, and it bears the influence of both Andrew Jackson Downing and Calvert Vaux. This constituted a striking departure from the more formal, European style of landscape design, which favored orderly, symmetrical layouts and pathways with straight lines that evoked a sense of order and control over nature. This road, by contrast, follows the natural lay of the land.

David Huntington, the Man Who Saved Olana

So much of American culture has been distilled in tangible form, visible form, at Olana. . . . Olana was a totality, a concretion of the American spirit of a certain moment. And it wasn't just Frederic Church. It was us; it was we. It was as much America as, say, Versailles is France, which is not only Louis the Fourteenth; it's also Frenchness of a certain moment. . . . I think Versailles is a great monument as an expression of the spirit that tells us a great deal about a culture in a certain stage of its development. And that's how I feel about Olana, that it is a mirror of where we've been. It's a way-station along the history of our sense of identity, as is Monticello, as is Mount Vernon.

—DAVID HUNTINGTON

David Carew Huntington. Faculty and staff biographical files, Smith College Archives, Smith College Special Collections, Northampton, Massachusetts.

David Huntington was a forty-two-year-old art historian teaching at Smith College when he got the news that Sally Good Church had died and Olana—the land, the house, and all its contents—were about to be sold or auctioned off, including hundreds of works by Church; dozens of paintings by Hudson River School artists; and Italian, Spanish, French, and Flemish Old Masters Church had collected over the course of his life.

Sally was the widow of Church's youngest son, Louis; when she died in 1964 Huntington was the world's leading expert on her father-in-law, but when she met him a decade earlier he was still a graduate school student who was intensively studying the work of an almost entirely forgotten American painter.

In 1953 Huntington was invited for lunch with Sally, who by this time was frail and suffering from dementia. The staff at Olana knew that the young scholar wanted to examine the collection and spend meaningful time inside the house, so they told him: *Park your car out of sight at the edge of the woods, and after lunch say goodbye and leave by the front door.* Then, moments later, he reappeared, as instructed, at the back door and was escorted up a rear stairway into the attic, where he was "staggered" to discover a treasure trove. In addition to the huge collection of artworks, journals, and prints, there were thousands of photographs that would, many years later, come to be seen as one of the most important collections of nineteenth-century photography.

Huntington also uncovered "many trophies," as a newspaperman described them in 1869, including "a Bedouin Arab's spear, a suite of Damascus armor, a huge bit of the Parthenon, Turkish embroidery, Palestine beads, etc., etc." He later called the place "a Yankee gentleman's Noah's Ark of all that civilization had to offer the New World . . . crammed full of the painter-architect's sketches, letters, diaries, and any kind of memorabilia one can think of, including a traveler's collapsible set of flatware, and canceled checks to Brooks Brothers."

Rummaging through Church's home that day, David Huntington embarked on what would become one of the most important projects in the story of American art. Whoever comes to Olana and also falls in love with this place owes him the greatest debt of gratitude.

Frederic Church enjoyed extraordinary fame and fortune during his lifetime, but his work, along with that of his fellow Hudson River School painters, had fallen out of favor by the time he died in 1900, when art lovers preferred more avant-garde European art. As Huntington was writing his graduate school dissertation he was constantly confronted with patronizing comments from professors who believed "I was wasting my time working on a Hudson River School painter." But he continued to think about, and study, Church's work, and he had the good fortune at Smith to find a new generation that was also intrigued by the painter/architect's work.

Understanding the priceless cultural value of Olana's holdings, Huntington had made an informal agreement with the estate's executor, a lawyer and Sally Church's nephew, Charles Lark, that he would be notified when Sally died so he could help launch a campaign to save the estate. But that didn't happen, as Huntington learned, to his horror, when a fellow art historian shared the contents of a telegram he had just received, referring to Church's last will and testament: SEE OLANA THIS WEEKEND OR NOT AT ALL | THE EXECUTORS ARE DETERMINED TO LIQUIDATE THE ESTATE | SELL THE CONTENTS OF THE HOUSE AT AUCTION AS QUICKLY AS POSSIBLE AFTER | WILL ADMITTED TO PROBATE NEXT WEEK.

Huntington immediately returned to Olana and "began desperately photographing it." He helped mobilize a broad group of supporters to join the battle to save the estate, which included academics, politicians, museum professionals, members of prominent Hudson Valley families, New York City millionaires, and cultural leaders. Philip Johnson and Lincoln Kirstein paid rent on the estate as the group raced against the clock. Journalists and historians wrote articles introducing Church's work to a public that had entirely forgotten him; a major exhibition of paintings, oil sketches, drawings, and personal memorabilia opened at the Smithsonian; and an organization named Olana Preservation, Inc., was founded in March 1965, which raised enough money to purchase the entire property from the estate of Sally Good Church and save it from being sold.

But it was David Huntington who had put the wheels in motion. His *Landscapes of Frederic Edwin Church: Vision of an American Era*, the book version of his dissertation, was instrumental in reintroducing Church's art, which he cast as a story about America. Tying Church to the Transcendentalist movement and the writings of Ralph Waldo Emerson, Henry David Thoreau, and Walt Whitman, Huntington presented his paintings as an expression of what he saw as a new tide of patriotism that would "celebrate the newness of this vast, half-claimed continent." He saw Olana as "a domestic cathedral of the Transcendentalist mystique of American destiny: the New World as the meeting of East and West, civilization and nature."

In an era of exponential growth that included farming, manufacturing, and heavy industry; the expansion of the American homeland to include Texas, much of the Southwest, California, Oregon, and Washington; and a new network of railroads, canals, and steamships to connect the disparate parts of the growing economy, a new sense of what it meant to be an American was beating in the hearts of artists, writers, philosophers, businesspeople, and politicians. Historian David Seamon explains that like many of his contemporaries, Church believed that "America was destined to become a great country and that its geographic expansion and economic development were God-given truths. This expansionist impulse—most commonly called 'Manifest Destiny'—became an important theme for Church and other Hudson River School painters." It was Huntington who located Frederic Church at the center of this transformation, writing that "his artist's hand held the pulse of a generation." Borrowing a phrase from Thoreau, Huntington added that, alone among American painters, Frederic Church had experienced "total immersion in nature." He was "an archetypal American," and Olana, his greatest creation, was an American treasure that had to be saved.

On June 27, 1966, Governor Nelson Rockefeller landed in a helicopter at Olana to sign an act of the legislature that allowed New York State to acquire title to the entire property from Olana Preservation and operate it as a museum and public park. One of the most critical yet underappreciated factors in the saving of Olana was the longevity of Sally Good Church. As Robert Toole observes in the *Historic Landscape Report*, the entire property "might well have been quickly sold and eventually dismantled" if it hadn't been for her. Sally's long life—she died in August 1964 at the age of ninety-six—allowed public sentiment toward preservation to evolve in favor of saving the entire property, both the house *and* the landscape, for the future.

The whole colorful story was recounted in an oral history interview conducted by Charles Hosmer Jr. in 1988 and memorialized by Dorothy Heyl in a

Governor Nelson Rockefeller (left) and David Huntington in the bell tower at Olana, June 27, 1966. Photo courtesy of the Register-Star/Columbia-Greene Media.

pamphlet titled *The Campaign to Save Olana*, which is available for sale in the park's store. I sat down with Heyl, the leading expert on Huntington, in early 2025 to ask what she believes are the most important things a visitor should know and understand about him. I suggested, at the beginning of our conversation, that in the twentieth century story of American preservation Huntington's name ought to be much better known, along with, for example, Joshua David and Robert Hammond, the men who led a long David-and-Goliath fight to save the High Line in New York City and transform it into a public park.

Dorothy Heyl reminded me that the fight save Olana began at a time when historic preservation was just coming into vogue and Penn Station was still standing. She credits Huntington with "almost single-handedly resurrecting Church's reputation as one of America's great painters." From the moment he learned that Olana and all its contents were going to be sold off, Heyl said, he "embarked on this quixotic mission, guided only by his conviction that Olana must be saved." She told me Huntington made so many phone calls—to curators, art historians, and potential donors—that the IRS suspected he was running a gambling operation.

What David Huntington understood before anyone else, Heyl added, was that "the castle on the hill, filled with a forgotten artist's stuff, might have seemed like a white elephant in a postwar booming economy, but he recognized that it was a *gesamtkunstwerk*—a total work of art." It had been "miraculously preserved" after Church's death, and he was determined to save it for future generations. In a speech at Olana right after Rockefeller's dramatic helicopter landing, Huntington wryly told the gathering of notables how glad he was that he no longer had to explain to friends that "Olana is not a girl, or a Hawaiian drink or an illegal drug (although one of my friends thinks Olana may replace LSD)."

Today a New York State Historic Site and National Historic Landmark, Olana opened to the public in 1967.

The Indispensable Partnership

The first national historic preservation organization in the United States is considered to be the Mount Vernon Ladies' Association, which formed in 1853 to save George Washington's home. The effort began after Louisa Bird Cunningham passed by the house one evening and was alarmed by its shabby appearance. According to the official Mount Vernon website, she wrote a letter to her daughter, Ann Pamela Cunningham, and "made the comment that if the men of the United States would not save the home of its greatest citizen, maybe the women should do it." Ann Pamela was galvanized into action and organized the Mount Vernon Ladies' Association with the goal of saving the home of the nation's first president.

Cunningham's group, which included one woman vice regent for every state in the union, raised the funds necessary to purchase the entire estate and, in 1860, opened it to the public. Although the Mount Vernon Ladies' Association was not the kind of formal public/private partnership that would become common in the twentieth century, the women of Mount Vernon pioneered the idea of private citizens taking responsibility for preserving and managing a historically important place. It was also the first campaign to preserve not only a historic house but also an entire site, including outbuildings, grounds, and vistas.

One hundred years later, as time was running out to save Olana, a similar, optimistic spirit filled the Court Hall when a group of private citizens who had organized as Olana Preservation, Inc., came together with the task of raising almost $200,000 toward the total purchase price of $479,000 that had been set by the estate's executor, Charles Lark. Even though the entire 250 acres, including the artist-designed landscape, house, and collection, had been designated a National Historic Landmark, its fate was still insecure. By January 1966, having already raised thousands of dollars, the group had just five months left to save Frederic Church's home from being sold. Led by Alexander Aldrich, a cousin of Rockefeller's, the people in the room that day were a mix of local citizens committed to protecting Olana; artists, historians, and preservationists; and politically and socially connected individuals. Even after the legislation to preserve Olana had been signed on June 27, the trustees understood it would take months before state funding would materialize, and the executor had set a June 30 deadline to receive his purchase price. At this point some of the officers took out personal loans to make up the difference,

The Court Hall at Olana, looking toward the front door, with the word "Welcome" in Arabic, 1969. Photographer unknown. Courtesy National Park Service.

and Olana Preservation succeeded in purchasing the estate. Thus it was that a group of private citizens held title to Frederic Church's home before it was transferred to the State of New York.

Once they had saved the estate, a new challenge arose: to maintain, interpret, and make meaningful this immense, unique work of art for future generations. In 1971, Historic Site Manager Dick Slavin organized Friends of Olana, a private nonprofit that built on the work of Olana Preservation and worked in collaboration with the New York State Office of Parks, Recreation and Historic Preservation (NYS Parks). The Friends group dedicated itself to supplementing the state's resources through fundraising and advocacy; working with NYS Parks to restore the landscape and house; and creating public programs that would spread awareness and enthusiasm for the work of Frederic Church—both as artist and landscape architect—and provide a window into the life of the Church family at Olana. The group's new independent legal status also gave it standing in the first major viewshed battle Olana would face: a proposed nuclear power plant across the Hudson River in Cementon.

Another thirty years later, the board of trustees voted to change the name again, to The Olana Partnership (TOP). Under its first president, Sara Griffen, this new name held great significance, indicating that the organization had evolved from a "friends group" dedicated mainly to supporting the staff and priorities of NYS Parks into an entity dedicated to advocating for Olana alongside the state agency and in close partnership with it. TOP hired staff—curators, educators, a cultural landscape specialist, an archivist, and marketing people—who enabled them to greatly expand their work in developing educational programs; supporting the work of scholars and journalists; undertaking preservation and conservation projects; commissioning art exhibitions; creating webinars, lectures, publications, and art exhibitions; and doing the crucial fundraising needed to support all those activities.

When I asked Linda Cooper, regional director for NYS Parks, about the

An artistically preserved hinge remnant on a felled tree.

agency's role in the partnership and what is involved in managing a site like Olana, she told me "it takes people, time, and funding." But sometimes, she continued, "it seems it takes a wave of a fairy godmother's wand as well." The parks crew has a wide and varied role that touches every inch of the property, from mechanical systems onsite—fire suppression, heat, ventilation, HVAC, and septic—to the many rooms in Church's house. Parks staff go through each one and meticulously wipe down artifacts and furniture; they clean fabrics, scrub and shine floors, and repair leaks and parts of the structure that may have broken—a pane of glass knocked down by the wind or a stone wall that needs repointing. They have an administrative role as well that spans everything from human resources to legal affairs.

NYS Parks staffers have offices at Olana alongside their colleagues in TOP, and also work on exhibits, loans, academic writing, and large initiatives like a digitization project that will cover the expansive Church archive of paintings and drawings. Visitors will often see crews working in the landscape, mowing lawns and meadows and caring for the carriage roads, especially after heavy rains. Sometimes a big storm topples a tree along one of the drives, or leaves one hanging precariously over a path, and workers with chain saws arrive in trucks bearing the distinctive green maple leaf logo of the New York State Parks system, "Estd. 1924." I often stop to chat with these groundskeepers, who are happy to pause their work and describe what species of tree has died and how old it likely was. They clear away branches and parts of the trunk that could present a tripping hazard or obstruct an electric vehicle, but otherwise the Parks crew leaves dead and dying trees in the forest, a gesture that is both friendly to wildlife and also in keeping with Frederic Church's artistic vision of the naturalistic landscape. Sometimes their work results in its own work of art; I once overheard a fellow walker near the Olana lake observe that a recently felled tree left a pattern on its stump that ingeniously resembled the Manhattan skyline.

Frederic Church visited George Washington's home two years before Ann Pamela Cunningham launched her campaign to save it, and he left behind a handsome sketch of the walled enclosure, arched entrance, and iron gate of the president's tomb at Mount Vernon. Much of the work that Olana's preservationists would begin to do, six decades after the artist himself died, was to ensure that his home would, like Mount Vernon, be preserved as a cultural monument to an important part of the American story.

For a visitor to Olana, what is meaningful to remember is that we are all walking in the footsteps of David Huntington and countless individuals who have worked since the 1960s to engage the public in the story of Olana and preserve it—work that continues today through this vibrant, indispensable public/private partnership.

The Frederic Church Center for Art and Landscape

One of the first things landscape curator Mark Prezorski said when he welcomed Olana supporters to the groundbreaking ceremony for the Frederic Church Center for Art and Landscape was that the building was both sited and designed to be invisible. It's a remarkable statement for a place that celebrates the work of one of America's leading visual artists, but it's something I'm pretty sure Frederic Church would agree with. The idea was to blend the building into the landscape without allowing it to interfere with the natural features

The Frederic Church Center for Art and Landscape as it sits in the landscape.

Church used to compose views throughout the property. Nestled in a wooded area underneath Red Hill, you could easily drive right past it.

It wasn't until years after Prezorski's tour that I understood what he meant about the siting. Summoning the adventurous spirit of those fearless tree climbers of the Hudson River School, I clambered up the steep hill behind the new center and shimmied up a very tall dead white pine that had tipped over, roots and all, its crown resting on another tree just behind it. Now, from this aerial perch, it was possible to appreciate how the handsome building, with its dark red siding and flat, sloping roof, was tucked away into the crook of the hills that surround it on two sides.

The center was designed by the Architecture Research Office in collaboration with Nelson Byrd Woltz Landscape Architects, the firm that, a decade earlier, had helped developed a comprehensive master plan to restore or rehabilitate the entire 250-acre estate, including iconic viewscapes, native plantings, the farm complex, orchards, pastures, and historic house. The new building elegantly yet understatedly welcomes people as they round the first bend of South Road. Until recently visitors had been greeted at Church's colorful, fanciful, castle at the top of the hill, but over the past decade or so the emphasis has shifted from the famous house to the picturesque landscape he created here, and the new center is a gateway to understanding the rich, diverse history that lives in this place.

Inside, a giant screen—it was chosen because it's similar in size to *Heart of the Andes* and can display Church's great paintings at full scale—plays a video introduction to Frederic Church and his work and legacy beneath massive, crisscrossing wooden beams. You might find a group of seniors playing cards at one of the café tables, or a child running her finger up and down the soft, beige-colored interior walls that are lined with felt made from recycled wool. The acoustics are ideal for lectures and presentations, but also for sitting quietly with a cup of coffee and a book or gazing at the scenery outside an expansive wall of windows that offer majestic views of the Catskills. The room continues outside in a series of terraced gardens and a small amphitheater. Follow the stone steps up the hill, and you are greeted with one of Church's most splendid composed views: a lake encircled by trees, with the colorful house in the distance, perched at the top of a hill.

The all-electric, carbon-neutral building was designed to reduce Olana's overall carbon footprint and was built with environmentally friendly alternatives to concrete and steel. It was the first public building in New York State constructed as a mass timber project, using engineered wood products to form strong structural elements. Its interior beams are glue-laminated, and the exterior siding is Accoya wood made from Monterey pine (*Pinus radiata*), a sustainable product that resists damage from water, insects, and fungi. It was painted in a shade of red inspired by Olana's farm buildings.

But my favorite feature is the bird-friendly Ornilux glass that was installed in every window. Take a close look and you will see a spiderweb pattern embedded in the glass, a technology inspired by actual spiders, which weave ultraviolet-reflective strands of silk into their webs to prevent birds from flying into and destroying them. The glass is virtually transparent to the human eye, unless you press your nose up to the glass. Here is a feature in the contem-

A winter view of Olana.

porary landscape that Church, an ardent bird lover, would have robustly applauded. In letters from his travels around the world the artist described in colorful detail the "multitudes" of birds he saw, from monstrously huge pelicans and "man of war hawks" to "small bright green parrots" and parakeets. "I heard some sweet songs," he wrote to his mother from Colombia. He painted and sketched birds throughout his life, including in his most celebrated paintings, like *Heart of the Andes* (1859), *Cotopaxi* (1862), and *Chimborazo* (1864). In fact, Gerald Carr, who spearheaded the Church *Catalogue Raisonné*, notes that in his student exercise book while at the Hartford Grammar School, young Frederic made drawings of eagles in flight and an owl on a perch, images Carr deems "the earliest productions by Church that may be considered works of art." After he made his home at Olana Church and his family cared for the many birds who lived in and passed through the landscape on their migrations. Outside Cosy Cottage was an elaborate bird feeder, and tins of exotic bird food—probably the "Indian meal dough" Church referred to in an 1888 letter—were discovered during archeological research in the 1990s.

Bird-friendly glass is just one example of the many ways, some visible, some less so, that the contemporary stewards of this place are endeavoring to carry on the much earlier work of nineteenth century environmentalists who shared Church's reverence for the natural world and influenced his thinking about conservation and preservation.

Catskill Mountain House and the Roots of Landscape Tourism

At the same time Frederic Church was building his carriage drives at Olana, a new kind of road was being planned across the river: a funicular cable car that would climb thousands of feet up the Wall of Manitou and carry passengers to one of the most popular attractions on the East Coast: the Catskill Mountain House. The road was called the Otis Elevating Railway, and anyone who has ever ridden an elevator will recognize the name. Founded in 1853, the Otis Elevator Company has a long history of innovation and has been around long

The Otis Elevating Railway and, at top left, the Catskill Mountain House, ca. 1902. Detroit Publishing Co., Library of Congress.

enough to have both installed (in the 1880s) and later modernized (in 2002) the elevators in the Eiffel Tower. But it is less well-known for the cable system it created in the Hudson Valley that enabled one of the greatest tourism booms in America.

When this fancy wilderness resort opened in 1824, the only way to reach it was by a long, dusty, bone-shattering stage coach ride up the mountain. The Otis Elevating Railway opened in August 1892 and, for seventy-five cents, made a connection with the Catskill Mountain Railway. This line carried tourists from the Catskill wharf after they had disembarked from one of the popular Day Lines that traveled from New York City up the river that was often referred to as "America's Rhine," in the cradle of the Hudson Valley. These boats were speedy steamships that provided, along with stunning views, a luxurious experience that earned them the moniker "floating palaces." There were bands and orchestras to enliven the journey, and fine dining, barbershops, newsstands, and writing rooms. One boat was equipped with a darkroom so passengers who were practicing the new art of photography could develop and print their pictures on board.

The year 1824 marked a turning point in the tourism industry, following the US Supreme Court ruling in *Gibson v. Ogden*, which struck down a New

Illustration of the Catskill Mountain House, 1868, from Charles Sweetser's *Book of Summer Resorts*.

York State law that had granted a monopoly to the successor of the pioneering North River Steamboat Company, founded by Robert Livingston and Robert Fulton. In the aftermath of the ruling several new lines sprang into business, and, according to *The Tourist*, by 1830 there were eight lines operating twenty-nine steamboats on the Hudson River. Once the monopoly had been busted, the cost of a trip from New York City to the Catskill Mountain House saw a significant reduction, and tourism boomed. Commercial shipping also surged after the Erie Canal was completed in 1825 and opened a pathway to the western part of the developing nation, beginning a process that would transform the Hudson River into a transportation superhighway.

Frederic Church wore out many pair of boots hiking to the Mountain House, intensely studying and taking notes on his surroundings as he walked and sketched. The huge, bright white, colonnaded Greek Revival hotel was clearly visible from several spots at Olana, and it became a famous feature in the landscape; in June 1834, a woman traveling up the Hudson on the steamboat *Erie* noted in her journal that "the mountain house was seen like a white cloud in the midst of the blue ridge." By the time his Persian-inspired villa

Hudson River Day Line steamer *Albany* after passing under the Poughkeepsie Bridge, ca. 1900–1910. Detroit Publishing Co., Library of Congress.

at the top of the hill was ready for the family to start moving into the upper floors, Church's own house had become an attraction. As reported by the *Catskill Examiner* in August 1872, it was "one of the prominent things now pointed out to the tourists and travellers." If you visit the boat launch in the lovely Ernest R. Lasher Memorial Park in Germantown and look north from the edge of the Hudson River, you'll see Olana perched on its hill about five miles to the north, and you can imagine the thrill it must have given a passenger on one of the Day Liners.

The Catskill Mountain House resort—the first of several that would open along the Catskill peaks—was intentionally burned down in 1963, but the rock ledge it once stood on can still be seen from Olana, as can the route that was cut along the mountainside by the Otis Elevating Railway. The outdoor terrace at the Center for Art and Landscape offers a clear view of the site, especially when a dusting of snow covers the track of the old funicular line. It can also be seen from the top of Church Hill, near the main house, and from the seating area on Ridge Road.

The Name "Olana"

When I first started coming to Olana in the mid-1980s it was common knowledge that Olana meant "our place on high" in Arabic. It wasn't until years later, when I read an essay by the poet John Ashbery, who lived in Hudson and knew—and loved—Olana well, that I learned its real meaning. In his essay Ashbery explained the meaning of the name in both historic and personal terms, and he credits historian Gerald Carr with discovering the word "Olana" in a volume by the Greek geographer Strabo—a book Church had multiple editions of in his library, one of which was a Christmas gift from Isabel. *Olane*, Carr explains, was the name of "a fortress and 'treasure storehouse' not far from Artaxata, the ancient Persian capital on the Araxes (Aras) River which empties into the Caspian Sea." According to Ashbery, it was one of the supposed sites of the Garden of Eden.

"Doubtless this was the meaning Church had in mind," Ashbery writes: "a fortress to protect his fragile family (two children had died in infancy); a treasure house because it sheltered not just the glittering trophies he brought back from his travels but that family itself—his wife and their four surviving children." It is worthy of note that in recent years scholars have established it was Isabel Church who came up with the name Olana, perhaps having read the ancient text she had given to her husband.

The "Land" in Landscape

When the Europeans settled in the Hudson Valley in the early seventeenth century, the landscape of America was a mystery, a place they called "wilderness." Environmental historian Roderick Frazier Nash describes the Old World view of the forest as a threatening place filled with "demons and spirits," and our earliest ancestors made it their life's work to tame and conquer it.

In an essay introducing the 2024 *Native Prospects* show at the Thomas Cole Site, Scott Manning Stevens (Akwesasne Mohawk) writes about how "deeply problematic" the term "wilderness" is, because "to insist on North America, before the arrival of Europeans, as a wilderness is to vacate it of its indigenous inhabitants or demote them to the status of wild animals."

The artists in that striking exhibition dealt with the theme of erasure in various ways, my favorite of which was Kay WalkingStick's *Thom, Where Are the Pocumtucks (The Oxbow)*. WalkingStick (Cherokee), brings a wry sense of humor to her painting, which overlays a traditional Indigenous stenciled design onto the U-shaped river in Thomas Cole's famous 1836 *View from Mount Holyoke, Northampton, Massachusetts, after a Thunderstorm—The Oxbow*. The Pocumtucks once inhabited the Connecticut River valley in western Massachusetts but were long ago dispossessed of their lands; as a consequence of colonialism there is no Pocumtuck community today. The effect of her design, as WalkingStick explains it, "is to stop the eyes of the viewer and force them to see the pattern and to recognize that it is on top of the land," where it becomes a barrier that the viewer is forced to reckon with. Her intention with this riff on *The Oxbow*, she explained in an interview, is to show how "it is important to me on a deep level, on a spiritual level, that people understand that we are all living on Indian land, every one of us."

A small piece of sculpture by Alan Michelson (Mohawk member of the Six Nations of the Grand River), re-created the settler cabin in Cole's 1847 painting *Home in the Woods* and papered over the entire structure, including the steps that led to the front door, with the text and survey maps of the 1809 Treaty of Fort Wayne, which forced allied Native nations to surrender approximately three million acres of land to the United States for settlement and development. "Whereas Cole presents his viewer with an idyllic scene of domestic life in a woodland untroubled by territorial conflict," Manning Stevens comments in his essay, "Michelson pointedly reminds us of how such lands were forcibly taken by the United States and made available to Euro-American homesteaders."

Unlike his student Frederic Church, who almost never included an Indigenous figure in his paintings of North American landscapes, Thomas Cole did paint Native peoples into some of his works, but as Manning Stevens observes, they were designed as "staffage," simply an accessory to convey a sense of time and place. Today, just outside the site of Church's original studio on New Approach Road, a visitor will pass an interpretive sign about the Mohican people, which features *Pap-scan-ee*, a panoramic oil painting by the Native artist L. F. Tantillo. The painting depicts a Mohican summer encampment near the Hudson River, circa 1600, with the Catskill range in the background—an imaginative evocation of the people who lived, hunted, fished, and farmed on this land long ago.

Indigenous depictions of the land "reify our relationships and responsibilities" to it, Manning Stevens writes; "they call on us to be mindful of and thankful for those relationships and duties, rather than to claim proprietary rights over a sweeping panorama or the curated prospect of a country estate." These observations are good walking companions. As we wander through Olana and experience the many composed views made on this stunning, original, and inspiring "country estate," we can always do what Jo Harjo, a poet of the Muscogee Nation, so wisely counsels in her stirring 1983 poem: We can *remember.*

A border collie leads her humans along the gentle curve of South Road, late September 2025.

The North Road switchback, January 2019.

SECTION 2: NORTH ROAD, 1869

It is helpful to remember, as we embark on a walking tour at Olana, that the more than five miles of carriage roads Frederic Church built had two purposes: They were utilitarian, providing a route to the stables and farm, and they were pleasure drives, designed to create a totally new experience for guests and friends, the joy of moving through a landscape that itself is a work of art. North Road was the original entry point to Olana from the city of Hudson, just a few miles to the north, and for many years, until the New Approach Road was completed around 1888, it was the way most visitors arrived at Church's estate.

Having left the city behind, Church's visitor plunged into what one historian called "a picturesque grove of hundred-year-old hemlocks." Most of the original trees are gone, but a dense forest remains, and the terrain here is ragged and wildly uneven; it is a part of the Olana property that looks like it was cut and splintered by a glacier, which left behind deep gashes in the rolling hillside and plenty of erratics, those leftover boulders from the last ice age, scattered hither and yon.

The first section of North Road bifurcates the landscape, with a high meadow on the western side and the unruly forest to the east. The road curves gently here, but enough to hide the path ahead, so you can't see beyond the next curve until you get there. Church could have laid out this section of road in a straightaway, which likely would have taken less time and money. Instead he did what his fellow landscape artists Calvert Vaux and Frederick Law Olmsted had recently done in Central Park: Following the aesthetic guidance of Andrew Jackson Downing, he crafted the opening segment of North Road so it would romantically meander through the landscape toward his farm. After a quarter of a mile there is a fork in the road, with Farm Road continuing in a straight line toward Cosy Cottage and the historic farm and North Road making a hairpin turn up the hill.

By planting hundreds of trees in this forest, Church designed an experience that would be rich with mystery and contrasts: shadow and light, glimpses of meadow on the other side of steep, rocky, hills, with constant changes of direction on the compass—heading north, then south, then north, then south again, for several rounds until the path intersects with Ridge Road at the top of hill and a whole new experience begins. Walking along North Road might cause a modern visitor to marvel, as one of Church's contemporaries did, at "the expenditure of road-building, and in otherwise bringing this huge, wild, steep mass of earth into suitable shape and condition." This person, a reporter named Zabriskie who visited Olana in 1884, commented that none of this could be accomplished "by the Bohemian type of artist, whose wealth is in purely aesthetic securities and whose castles are all in Spain." From his perch at the top of the North Road switchback, Zabriskie observed that "the hill is very precipitous here, and one looks down at times . . . [into] an almost inaccessible gulf." This was the dramatic entry to Church's Olana, designed to bestow a sense of awe and wonder in a natural landscape unlike any other.

"Donkey Fever"

When you arrive at the fork in North Road, you'll find a delightful photo taken in October 1884, enlarged on a signpost. It shows Church's mother-in-law, Emma Carnes, and her granddaughter Isabel Charlotte, known as Downie, riding in a farm wagon pulled by a milk-white donkey.

In 1869, having survived a brutal storm at sea during their sixty-nine-day crossing, a small group of white donkeys who hailed from Damascus and Baghdad arrived in Hudson, New York. The animals had "bruised bodies" but were otherwise robust and ready for their new assignment. In a letter to his friend William Henry Osborn, Church called them "the genuine Bagdaddians," graced with "a most superb gait." According to Isabel Church, the white donkey was "the most delightful beast she ever rode." It was only a few weeks their arrival that Church declared "a donkey fever is growing in this neighborhood." One of them, he boasted, is "fat and sleek and as domestic as a dog" and had already claimed a medal at the Catskill County Fair. "They are wonderful creatures," Church wrote to another friend, a delight to the entire family, and they were outfitted in "festive green coats and red harnesses" that Emma Carnes had helped to fashion. It wasn't long before the Syrian donkeys became one of the great treasures of Olana, escorting friends and family through the landscape that Church was busy designing.

The photograph on North Road is a reminder that he wanted his visitor to experience this landscape in motion. We are meant to move *through* it, and no matter how many times you come here, the experience will be different as so many factors—weather, light, season, time of day, the conversation of your walking companion—work their subtle effects on your journey.

As you huff and puff up the hill, you might have to step aside for another type of carriage: a Global Electric Motorcar, or GEM, that replaced the donkeys in the early part of the twenty-first century. Painted white in tribute to their Syrian predecessors, these vehicles now escort visitors along the carriage roads so they can have the Olana experience in precisely the way that Frederic Church conceived in the 1860s.

Isabel Charlotte (Downie) Church and her grandmother, Emma Carnes. NYS Parks.

Downie Church

Before you continue on your hike up North Road, have a good look at the photograph of Isabel Charlotte Church. Here is another artist in the Church family, one whose work is only recently gaining the attention it deserves. Downie (she got the nickname as an infant, because her fuzzy hair reminded her parents of a baby chick, and she kept it for the rest of her life) was an accomplished botanical artist. In Olana's collection are more than 140 of her illustrations, ranging from watercolors and pencil and ink drawings to oils on canvas. They were first exhibited in 2021 in the nationally touring exhibition *Cross Pollination: Heade, Cole, Church, and Our Contemporary Moment.* Like her father and his teacher, Thomas Cole, Downie's artworks contain handwritten notes made from her observations in the field. She began making watercolors of plants when she was an adolescent, practicing the same keen art of observation and faithfulness to detail so prized by her father.

To illuminate Downie's artistry in a webinar, Olana curator William Coleman displayed her watercolor study of goldenrod, made in September 1890, when she nineteen. This drawing, Coleman observed, is an example of the "rigorous scientific vision" of an artist who is "trying to capture the specifics of this particular plant in its living reality." Rather than "trying to evoke vast landscapes and narratives around it," Coleman went on, Downie focused her skilled hand and artist's eye on the plant's morphology and individual characteristics, in an effort, as he said, "to capture it as it is."

Goldenrod filled the meadows of Olana each autumn of Downie's life, and it still does. The Olana collection currently has more than one hundred examples of her work, including twenty-nine watercolors that were recently donated by Downie's great-granddaughter: stunningly beautiful, precise botanical paintings of staggerbush (known in Downie's time as *Andromenda mariana*), wild black currant (*Ribes floridum*), eastern smooth beardtongue (*Penstemon laevigatus*), red-berried elder (*Sambucus racemosa*), "Chain of Love" (Cadena de Amor), and more. She was a supremely gifted artist who was also working at Olana, and her oeuvre is slowly, but finally, emerging in exhibitions.

Andrew Jackson Downing

"I am busy landscape architecturing," Frederic Church wrote in an 1887 letter. Here he reveals the influence of Andrew Jackson Downing, the father of landscape gardening in America and a visionary who saw road building as a form of art.

Any visitor who walks a carriage road at Olana will feel the hand of Downing guiding her around bends in the road, a feature that offers the gift of discovery and mystery. Downing favored roads and pathways that follow the natural curves of a landscape and present visitors with different views and perspectives as they walk along. If, as you wander through Olana, you find yourself recalling a walk through the Ramble or North Woods Trails in Central Park, there's a reason: Downing was also an inspiration to Frederick Law Olmsted and Calvert Vaux, and the same Romantic spirit animated those places, with gestures intended to convey a sense of anticipation at what we might encounter around the next bend. Vaux, whom Church hired for architectural help on the house at Olana, was Downing's protégé, and his "landscape-driven design approach," as Sean Sawyer described it, clearly had enormous appeal to Church.

In his *Treatise on the Theory and Practice of Landscape Gardening*, Downing articulated his love for asymmetry and the use of irregular and natural forms. The "genius of the place" is found in diversity—or, as Downing put it, "infinite variety"—as we move from "wild" to "picturesque." Unifying it all is the "chief beauty of curved and bending lines in walks." In his library Church had a copy of Vaux's book *Villages and Cottages*, published in 1857, and there are echoes of Downing—who had died five years earlier in a steamship accident—throughout. "The great charm in the forms of natural landscape lies in its well-balanced irregularity," Vaux wrote, and "roads should wind in graceful, easy curves." These are perfect descriptions of the carriage roads Church would build at Olana, and while no evidence has yet been found that Church actually owned or had read the famous *Treatise*, it is beyond doubt that he was influenced by Downing and that

The letter “A” introducing the word “Architecture” in Andrew Jackson Downing’s *Treatise*.

he and Vaux were deeply engaged in conversations about his philosophy of landscape design.

Downing was a key popularizer of “the Picturesque” in America, which became a defining artistic style of nineteenth-century Romantics like the Hudson River School painters. The aesthetic had first been articulated by the English travel writer William Gilpin, who published a book praising the wild scenery of Wales in 1782. This scenery was considered “picturesque,” Elizabeth Barlow Rogers explains, “in that it could be viewed according to the same compositional principles found in painting.” For Downing the two fields, landscape gardening and painting, were closely allied, and Olana is among the world’s most perfect manifestations of his philosophy. Robert Toole, the landscape architect, offers the simplest and, to my ear, clearest definition of what “Picturesque” meant in the nineteenth century: “natural in appearance without pretensions.” What Church accomplished, Toole observes, was to induce “a sense of repose and reverie for nature and country life, all within the modest artifice of a gentleman’s farm.”

But the word “picturesque” also had a personal meaning to Church. In an 1871 letter to his great friend William H. Osborn he described how his three children were carried along Olana’s carriage roads on their donkey, with Winnie and Louis in "basket panniers" on either side of the animal and Freddie riding in the middle. Together "they present a jolly appearance, highly picturesque," he wrote, showing that in the landscape his own family, and the way in which they used and passed through it, were also picturesque.

Foremothers

As you ascend the steep, serpentine path of North Road, you will be taking a walk through time. The beginnings of this hill, technically called a rock drumlin, probably began more than twenty thousand years ago, when a thick, heavy, and probably quite noisy glacier spread south from Labrador into the Hudson Valley. "It's a giant bulldozer," Robert and Johanna Titus, who call themselves "the Catskill Geologists," write; "it scrapes and it scours; it fractures, and it grinds the landscape below." Later, when the glaciers melted, they produced massive volumes of water that continued the process of eroding and sculpting the landscape. North Road snakes through the hilly terrain, and as you walk along you'll see remnants of the glacier—boulders, ledges, even pieces of stone embedded in the road—that remained after Frederic Church's men blasted their way up the hill while making this carriage road. The path cuts through these ancient glacial remains under a canopy of trees that are in varying stages of their life cycle: some clipped in half at the top, others eaten by insects, then bored by woodpeckers, and a large number in full, splendid leaf.

At the top of the hill, where North Road intersects with Ridge Road, you'll come upon a tree that unfailingly reminds me of the great nineteenth-century artist Susie M. Barstow, a very tall, stately, dead white pine that has a beautiful structure, almost like a piece of sculpture. It reminds me of a drawing Barstow made on a recently discovered letter that depicts five women climbing a spindly ladder they propped up against a dying pine tree so they could get a fine view of the Kaaterskill high peak. At the top, in skirts and traveling hat, Barstow has placed herself next to the initials S. M. B.

I first encountered Susie M. Barstow at the Thomas Cole Site, where the curatorial staff have dedicated themselves to introducing the female canon of the Hudson River School in exhibits like *Remember the Ladies: Women of the Hudson River School* and *Women Reframe Landscape: Susie M. Barstow and Her Circle*. When I saw Barstow's paintings for the first time I felt astonishment and intense joy. It was like discovering an Old Master. How, I wondered, did I get to middle age without knowing the work of this painter? I went to college in the Hudson Valley, took art history courses, and still have my battered old copy of H. W. Janson's classic *History of Art*. I knew all about Church, Cole, Cropsey, McEntee, Kensett, and Gifford. But Susie Barstow? And her circle of fellow Hudson River School painters that included (in alphabetical order) Julie Hart Beers, Isabel Charlotte "Downie" Church, Emily Cole, Sarah Cole, Charlotte Coman, Edith Cook, Josephine Ellis, Eliza Greatorex, Elizabeth Jerome, Mary Blood Mellen, Eveline Mount, Harriet Cany Peale, Jane Stuart, Mary Josephine Walters, and Laura Woodward? They have been left out of the story of American art until very recently, which means that most art lovers have been denied a surprisingly large, striking, and diverse portfolio of work.

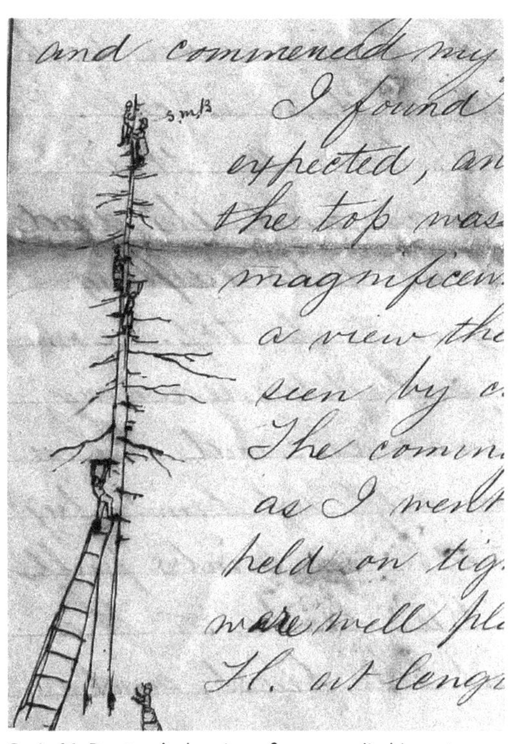

Susie M. Barstow's drawing of women climbing a tree. Courtesy Ken Barstow.

Many of these women were adventurers. Susie Barstow was an avid hiker who climbed at least 110 peaks, including in the Catskills, Adirondacks, and White Mountains in North America and the Alps, Tyrol, and Black Forest in Europe. She could do twenty-five miles in a day, and she sketched in the midst of blinding snowstorms. She painted in such cold temperatures that her watercolors froze on the page, "sometimes in little chunks of ice," and she would have to wait until she got home to thaw out her artworks. But what sets Barstow and her sisters apart from the men is that they climbed and hiked in long, heavy skirts with petticoats and corsets underneath. Nancy Siegel, who has written books and essays about Barstow, says she would pull her skirts up between her legs and use a "washing clip"—essentially a large clothespin—to anchor them, so she could maneuver more freely. But when a man came into view on the trail, down came the skirts—at least until he passed by. In 1877 the artist Mrs. W. G. Nowell lamented in an article titled "Mountain Suits for Women": "No wonder that gentlemen have been shy in asking us to accompany them in their explorations, for, in our ordinary attire, we must lag far behind, while they toil on ahead with double burdens, theirs and ours. Our dress has done all the mischief. It has kept us away from the glory of the woods and the grandeur of the mountain heights."

Susie Barstow in her hiking suit. Courtesy Ken Barstow.

My favorite painting of Inspiration Point in the Catskills—a beloved location of Hudson River School painters—is by Susie M. Barstow; it shows the rocky, jagged edges of the cliff with tall pines, some dying like the tree she and her friends used for their ladder, and a large bird of prey riding an air current directly toward the viewer. "I found it easier than I expected," Barstow wrote in that letter of her climb up the rickety ladder, "and when I reached the top I was repaid by a magnificent view all around."

Columbia-Greene Community College

If you hear joyous cheering or energetic music wafting through the woods to the east of North Road, it will no doubt be students from Columbia-Greene Community College a campus of the State University of New York that serves two counties on either side of the Hudson River. The act of preservation that saved Olana and established it as a historic site also set aside land for the creation of the college. The State of New York, in 1970, purchased 130 acres on the northeast boundary of Olana, a parcel that was once farmland owned by the Benham family. In the president's office is a lovely painting that shows a bucolic scene with the farmhouse and red barn that were here before the college campus was completed in the early 1970s.

The state also carved out a corridor of around twelve acres between the community college and North Road, creating a buffer between the two very different properties. The "wooded buffer" was an important element of the Romantic style of landscape gardening and it was a feature Church clearly loved, because he strategically planted native trees all over his property and used these thick woodlands to separate and define the different parts of his landscape: house, meadows, farm buildings, lake. In an 1867 letter he referred to this particular area, between North Road and the Benham farm, as "splendid woods," and today it remains so.

Columbia-Greene's president, Dr. Carlee Drummer, told me that since its founding the college, which serves a small rural population in a geographic area the size of Rhode Island, considers itself "the biggest little college in the world." She added that Columbia-Greene has been honored as a Leader College of Distinction by the national organization Achieving the Dream, which recognizes excellence in improving success outcomes and equity in a student population. In addition to a curriculum in the traditional liberal arts and sciences, the college offers workforce development programs in automotive technology, business, criminal justice, and nursing. Moreover, in an area the *Columbia Paper* called, in a 2025 front-page story, a "child care desert," Columbia-Greene operates a highly regarded Day Care Center for children ages

3–5 with a program that not only stimulates cognitive development and social and emotional growth but also provides a "living lab" for students majoring in early childhood education. For Drummer, this is a key part of the college's mission: to contribute to the economic stability of Columbia and Greene Counties by preparing students to meet the region's everchanging workforce needs.

Today The Olana Partnership and Columbia-Greene Community College work together in various ways, such providing the opportunity for students enrolled in U.S. history courses to examine artifacts and primary sources in The Olana archives. A certificate in Construction Technology and Preservation Carpentry, introduced in 2019, offers an internship program that provides a remarkable opportunity for students to contribute to the ongoing restoration of Frederic Church's historic house.

The college has a large, light-filled library that houses a vast collection of microfilm reels and bound print editions of local and regional newspapers going as far back as far as 1792. Columbia-Greene's librarian, Geralynn Demarest, told me that a recent donation from the archives of two regional papers was so large that the delivery required two tractor-trailers. My favorite spot in the college is the library's upstairs Olana Study Nook, a small, quiet space with comfortable chairs and a row of windows with a direct view toward North Road and the hill it climbs.

En Plein Air Painters

While artists have always sketched and painted outdoors, the invention of the tin paint tube in 1841 made it much easier for anyone to go out into the landscape with oil paints and sketch *en plein air*. Frederic Church worked in the field, as his teacher did, beginning with pencil sketches and employing Cole's practice of recording descriptions that detail the colors and atmospheric conditions he observed while working. On an 1890 panoramic pencil sketch showing a view of the mountains and Hudson Valley from his house, Church plotted the horizon points, marking the dates "Dec. 21st" and Jan 1" above two

Catskill peaks to indicate where the sun would set on those days. He scribbled notes directly onto his compositions, deployed numbered keys to correspond with entries that were noted in the margins, and created little observational maps that used words and images to remind him of what he saw, so when he returned to the studio he could faithfully reproduce them. Words like "brilliant," "dazzling," and "luminous" appear alongside color notations like "red orange" or "orange red," "purple" or "greenish." In *Sunset from Olana* he annotated his sketch with terms like "rich," "delicious," "smoky," and "dull."

In this practice we can locate the influence of Alexander von Humboldt, who urged artists to draw and paint "directly from nature" so that they might "reproduce the character" of different regions, foliage, trees, rocks, seashores, and even the soil in the forest. In an 1859 letter Church expressed his hope that his famous painting *Heart of the Andes* would be presented to Humboldt, and he described it as "a transcript of the scenery." Sadly, Humboldt died before having the chance to know Frederic Church's work or his profound influence on the artist.

A woman paints *en plein air*, her reflection echoed in the Olana lake.

Church usually traveled in the spring and autumn, making sketches that he would later turn into canvases in his studio in the winter. Historian Barbara Babcock Millhouse describes how he would arrange his sketches on a large table, "then move them about like pieces of a jigsaw puzzle to see how they could best be combined into a full-size painting."

Today at Olana a visitor will frequently encounter one or more painters with easels set up, working *en plein air* in the same way that Church and his colleagues did, often with umbrellas, stools, and rolling carts filled with their tubes of paint, brushes, palettes, and more. The Olana Partnership and NYS Parks welcome people of all ages and abilities into the landscape to paint, sketch and observe, and they are here throughout the year, in every season and type of weather, carrying on the tradition of *plein air* painting.

Frederic Church's composed view, looking west across the Hudson River to the Catskills.

SECTION 3: RIDGE ROAD, 1884

Oftentimes, while I am walking along one of entrance roads at Olana, a car will pull over, a window rolls down, and a person inside asks: *Do you know which is the best walk to take here?* I admit my answers can get a bit longwinded, but they always end up with same advice: *The most dramatic carriage road at Olana is Ridge Road,* and I point up the hill past the fortress-like castle that was Church's home. Revered for its grand, even breathtaking views of the Catskill Mountains and Hudson River, this road is rich with stories about the wider landscape and Olana's place in it.

Ridge Road begins just across the road from the Olana main house, and after a dozen or so yards you'll come to a fork in the path. Taking a hard right turn would lead you down the steep hill of North Road, with its many turns and switchbacks. But before you go any farther, look down at your feet; you'll notice that the gravel has a pinkish hue. This is shale that was imported from Pennsylvania because it most closely resembles the stone that came from Frederic Church's quarry at the very bottom of Red Hill. Church laid this stone along the five miles of carriage roads he built, and there is a patch at this point where the two roads meet—a reminder of what these "red-veined" pathways looked like in Church's day.

The best spot to appreciate the imposing knife edge of the Olana ridgeline is from the Rip Van Winkle Bridge, where you can take in the entire expanse of it from a distance. On Ridge Road itself, near the spot where the path intersects with Bethune Road, the view down the ridge is even more dramatic, as the steep cliff plunges in an almost vertical drop toward the state highway and Hudson River below. This untouched part of the Olana landscape is magical, mysterious, intimate, and at the same time terrifying. It never fails to induce a sense of awe.

Composing a View

One of Frederic Church's most magnificent composed views greets you as you round the first bend of Ridge Road. To the northeast, past a sweeping meadow with native grasses and wildflowers that cascade down a long hill, you can see the Berkshires of Massachusetts and the Green Mountains of Vermont. A bit closer is the Taconic Range, and as you pan to the north you will see Mount Merino, a handsome relic of the last ice age that virtually all the Hudson River School artists loved to paint or sketch. In the middle distance, just a few miles away, church spires rise from the city of Hudson.

Here's an idea to meditate on as you stroll along, with a dense, tall forest on one side and meadow, city, and mountain views on the other: This is a panorama that Frederic Church wanted you to see. After he purchased this parcel of some fifty acres in 1878, Church took the meadow, which had once been used for hay fields and grazing, out of production, fenced it off, and turned it into a rustic kind of parkland. Practicing the art of landscape gardening, he planted some trees himself, and in other areas allowed for second growth trees to emerge naturally. Without an agricultural purpose, Ridge Road was a purely ornamental road, and Church borrowed the many features in his landscape to compose a series of views for a visitor as he guided them around bends in the path, using trees and natural landforms as a way of framing those views, treating the entire landscape itself as a work of art. It was when he was laying out Ridge Road that he wrote to Erastus Dow Palmer, "I can make more and better landscapes in this way than by tampering with canvas and paint in the studio."

Becraft Mountain

Directly across from the east-facing picnic area on Ridge Road is what the Columbia County Historical Society deems a "geological wonder": Becraft Mountain. What makes this small earth form special is that it's one of just two outcroppings of the Catskill range (the other is Mount Ida). Becraft Mountain is made of the limestones of the Rondout and Manlius Formations—the same rock that forms the foundation of the Catskill Mountains. The escarpment dates to the Devonian era, almost four hundred million years ago. Frederic Church sketched and painted Becraft Mountain in the 1860s, and when he began mapping out Ridge Road in the early 1880s it became one of the borrowed views in his landscape.

Archeological findings show that as far back as the Paleo period 7,500 years ago, ancestral Mohican Indians were settled in the area around the Becraft escarpment. According to the Greenport Historical Society, long before the first white settlers arrived in the Hudson Valley, the chief of the Mohicans had his wigwam on the summit of Becraft Mountain, which provided a clear vantage point from which to survey the region and anticipate hostile attacks from the nation's longtime adversary, the Mohawks.

In *The Mohicans and Their Land: 1609–1730*, a remarkable book published in 1994, historian Shirley W. Dunn includes an appendix of 109 recorded transactions in which Dutch and later English settlers obtained Native American lands in the Hudson Valley. Some number of these deals were unfairly done by unscrupulous men, and the Indigenous peoples were cheated in many ways, not only from remuneration if, for example, they were not signatories to a deed, but also in the general expectation the Mohicans had that they would continue to have a right to fish and hunt on property they had sold—rights they were almost always denied.

Having pored over the transactions in Dunn's book and old maps of Columbia County, I believe it is plausible that the land around Becraft Mountain was part of Recorded Land Transaction No. 57, dated January 1, 1678, and made by four Indians: "Wattawit, for himself and his son, Appanewyett, and Sassioncha, sister of Wattawit, for herself and her little son Metschekamek." Interestingly, Dunn notes that women regularly appeared in Mohican deeds written by the Dutch and that "these relationships had to be addressed in Mohican land sales." We may never know which Mohican Indians lived, hunted, and farmed on Becraft Mountain, but one thing is sure: This was Indian land.

What makes this escarpment special in modern economic terms is "Becraft limestone," an essential component in the manufacture of Portland cement, the most common type of cement in use around the world. The little mountain's proximity to the Hudson River, less than four miles to the west, was a key factor in attracting the world's largest cement company, Atlas Portland Cement, to Hudson in 1910. Its Becraft Mountain plant employed eight hundred men who could produce 7,500 barrels a day, and it launched a century of heavy industry atop one of Olana's neighboring landforms.

In 1976 Atlas was purchased by St. Lawerence Cement, and two decades later the new company announced it was planning to build a massive, coal-burning plant atop Becraft Mountain with a forty-story tower that would have been the tallest structure between New York City and Montreal. Fired by five hundred million pounds of coal each year that would pulverize the Becraft limestone into Portland cement, the plume from a 406-foot stack would have extended for at least six miles. In an essay titled "The Bullet We Dodged," Sam Pratt, who helped lead the fight against St. Lawrence, noted the company sought permits to emit up to twenty million pounds of pollutants each year, including greenhouse gases, heavy metals and volatile organic compounds like arsenic, benzene, cadmium, chromium, lead, and mercury.

The Olana Partnership joined the fight to stop the plant as a consulting party in the legal process, and solicited testimony from art historians about the importance of protecting the views Frederic Church had composed at Olana. Many years later, in a conversation with me, longtime trustee Margaret Davidson reflected on the profound sense of responsibility The Olana Partnership felt to advocate for the *entire* viewshed of Olana, in all its richness and complexity, and recalled how the group made the case in public hearings that the 250-acre landscape Church created, along with the "borrowed views" he incorporated into this larger work of landscape art, were intended by the artist to be experienced as a whole. In April 2005, after a long, bitter engagement with the larger community and a ruling by New York's secretary of state that the project violated New York's coastal policies, St. Lawrence Cement abandoned the project.

Mount Merino

The little mountain—it's just a tad over five hundred feet in elevation—just to the north of Olana took its name from a breed of sheep that originated in Spain. They were first imported to the United States in 1802 by Robert R. Livingston. Livingston even published a book about the superiority of the Merino, "a kind of Shepherd's Manual," as he called it, that would "combine

Mount Merino, with the city of Hudson in the distance.

information and amusement" and help farmers understand the history of the breed and how to successfully raise the sheep. In the years that followed a Merino sheep craze swept through New York State and New England as fine wool—and the Merino sheep was said to have the finest wool of all—became an attractive investment. Several farmers raised Merino sheep on this shapely hill just to the north of Olana, which would become another of Church's borrowed views on Ridge Road. At one point there were as many as six hundred on one farm alone.

In scientific terms, Mount Merino is a rock drumlin, a bedrock hill that was sculpted and streamlined by passing glaciers during the last ice age. It is made up of bedded chert, better known as flint, which we encountered in our first footfalls at Olana when passing the quarry at Red Hill, and is part of the Normanskill Formation, a unit of rock that dates back around 450 million years ago to the Ordovician period. This little bedrock hill was sculpted into a particularly comely form, as geologists Robert and Johanna Titus observe: Its eastern and western slopes are steep and symmetrical, while the south slope, which is in view from Ridge Road, is elongated.

Frederic Church was known to love strange earth forms like this one; in Bogotá he wrote of hills and mountains that "rise in perpendicular masses like cathedrals" or "present corridors, domes and a variety of odd graceful forms." But he wasn't the only painter drawn to the natural beauty of Mount Merino, which appears in the sketches and paintings of many other artists, including Thomas Cole, Sanford R. Gifford, Asher B. Durand, Henry Ary, and Arthur Parton.

In the late 1990s, using conservation easements, the Columbia Land Conservancy preserved 122 acres of Mount Merino, and in 2008 Scenic Hudson, calling it "one of the most prominent features" in the Olana landscape, purchased and protected a further 102 acres. Today, in the open picnic area along Ridge Road, you'll often find a painter working *en plein air*, capturing a new view of this ancient, handsome little mountain. Another stunning view of Mount Merino that attracted the eye of many Hudson River School artists can be had looking south from Amtrak's lovely historic train station in Hudson.

The City of Hudson

The city of Hudson, nestled in the valley on the north side of Mount Merino, is a place of constant reinvention. The lands around it were originally home to the Mohican people, and on June 5, 1662, these River Indians sold a parcel that included the present-day city to a Dutchman named Jan Francen Van Hoesen for what the transaction recorded as "goods amounting to about 500 guilders in beavers." But the roots of the modern city begin in 1783, when a pair of brothers from one of Nantucket's most prominent whaling families came to what was then called Claverack Landing. There was a sentiment in those days, just after the American Revolution, that the British would not tolerate a permanent loss of the colonies, and, as Tim Mulligan puts it in his excellent guide to the Hudson River Valley, "they knew that their island home, out there in the Atlantic, would be particularly vulnerable in any new war coming from England. So they decided to find a safer place."

That place was Hudson, renamed in 1784 by the whalers who followed Seth and Thomas Jenkins. They sailed from Massachusetts, carrying the frames and lumber for the houses they would build once they arrived. They called

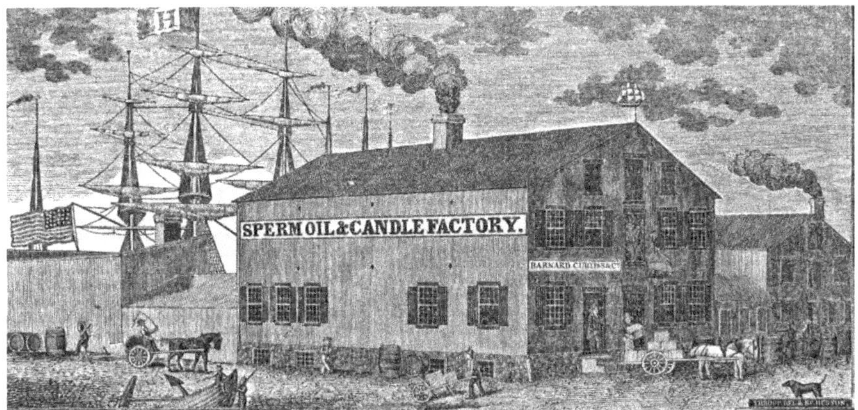

The Hudson Sperm Oil and Candle Factory, 1841, from the front page of *Rural Repository*, April 10, 1841.

themselves "the Nantucket Navigators"; today they are universally referred to as "the Proprietors," but as historian Margaret Schram points out, "*Entrepreneurs* would be the best word to describe them." These seafaring men who had lived most of their lives on an island some fifty miles from the mainland established one of the first grid systems of any American city. When Hudson was placed on the National Register of Historic Places in 1985, it was observed that the character of the original plan "has remained intact as an outstanding survival of early city planning and a dramatic representation of nineteenth-century governmental and cultural patterns."

Within just two years of its founding and blessed with a deepwater river harbor, the city of Hudson had become a commercial shipping behemoth, ranked second in the state behind New York City. Hudson merchants loaded their schooners, brigs, and sloops with a vast array of goods: butter, grains, vegetables, beeswax, and everything the slaughterhouses produced, from fresh horsemeat to smoked hams. They shipped forest products: hoops and staves for barrels, shingles, firewood, and boards for lumber. They also shipped pickled or smoked fish—herring, shad, and sturgeon—that were plentiful in the Hudson River.

Before long the city was humming with the many trades needed to support so much maritime commerce: sailmakers, blacksmiths, coopers, rope makers, caulkers, carpenters, and bakers specializing in "hard tack," the seafaring biscuit. There were men who kept the accounts in ledgers, chandlers who provided supplies for long voyages, and "carters" who made sure everything a ship needed was on board when it left port. In time new businesses arose: ice, candle, and soap factories, tanneries, and asheries that made potash from firewood ash. In the mid-nineteenth century the Hudson Iron Works, located in the bay between Mount Merino and the entrance to the city, converted crude ore into pig iron ready for use by manufacturers. This may have been the subject of Frederic Church's beautiful *Hudson River with Factory by Moonlight,* a haunting scene cast in shades of blue with sailboats on one side and a brick building with two stacks billowing white smoke on the other. The glacial activity that created the Hudson Valley also left abundant clay deposits along the riverbanks, which were ideal for brickmaking, another vibrant Hudson industry.

"The City of Hudson was a miracle," historian Schram writes. "Only the right combination of men with the right vision and business sense could have accomplished so much in such a short time." All of which they did in a small river town 120 miles from the sea.

ATHENS, FROM THE HUDSON IRON WORKS.

The Hudson Iron Works, reprinted from *The Hudson: From the Wilderness to the Sea,* by Benson J. Lossing, 1860.

In the decades since its founding, the city would reinvent itself multiple times: as a powerhouse in the cement industry, a magnet for artists and writers, an infamous red-light district, a mecca for the antiques business, a foodie heaven, and a longtime friend to the LGBTQ community. Hudson is known for having the best-preserved nineteenth-century main commercial street and "one of the richest dictionaries of architectural history in New York State," partly thanks to those early Nantucket settlers. The house of Robert Jenkins, son of Seth and a mayor of Hudson, is considered a fine example of Federal-style architecture. Located on lower Warren Street, it is open to visitors and has a library, small museum, and several important works of art, including Henry Ary's beautiful painting of Mount Merino.

As you stand on Ridge Road and look north toward the city, you'll see the large round dome above the county courthouse and several church spires. If you have a good pair of binoculars you might be able to see the clock face on the steeple of the First Presbyterian Church on Warren Street. One of the earliest examples of a public clock in nineteenth-century America, it was installed on October 9, 1802. When the church moved from its original location on Partition Street to a new, handsome Gothic edifice on Warren Street in 1837, the clock traveled too. It was placed in a tower at a much higher elevation, now visible and its bells marvelously audible from many areas in the landscape around it, including Ridge Road at Olana.

If you're wandering along this road at dusk you'll see the blaring guardtower lights of the Hudson Correctional Facility, a medium security prison for men. In the early twentieth century this was the New York Training School for Girls; it was here that a young Ella Fitzgerald was incarcerated after she was deemed to be "ungovernable." In April 1933 Fitzgerald managed to escape Hudson and made her way to the Apollo Theater in Harlem, where she entered an amateur night contest and began her career as a performing artist.

In addition to its vibrant arts, crafts, and food culture, Hudson still has an industrial footprint, as does Greenport, the town that encircles it. Looking east from Ridge Road you can see smokestacks and, between farm silos and forested areas, expansive, low-hung structures with huge parking lots—relics of the cement industry. The largest concerns today are a sustainable aquaculture firm, Hudson

Valley Fish Farm, which is currently the largest land-based commercial steelhead farm in North America; a massive stone quarry owned by A. Colarusso & Son on Becraft Mountain; and a flour mill owned by Archer-Daniels-Midland, which occupies a former cement plant and controls the rail line that passes through the urban center of Hudson and makes a connection to a loading dock on the river.

Hudson Hall

Hudson is also home to New York State's oldest surviving theater, the Hudson Opera House (renamed Hudson Hall in 2017), which in Frederic Church's time was a multipurpose civic institution known as City Hall that housed a post office, library, bank, and auditorium.

It was a vibrant, diverse place, hosting speakers like Henry Ward Beecher, Elizabeth Cady Stanton (her lecture was titled "Our Girls"), Susan B. Anthony, Horace Greeley, and Ralph Waldo Emerson. There were theatrical performances including *Uncle Tom's Cabin*, *Around the World in Eighty Days*, and *Corinne*. The famous Italian soprano Marietta Gazzaniga sang there in 1866, and "Blind Tom" Wiggins thrilled audiences at the piano twice in 1868 and again in 1871 and 1874.

In 1864, at the height of the Civil War, Frederic Church contributed a painting to the Sanitary Fair at Hudson Hall in support of Union troops, which was listed in the program simply as *Sunset*. Intriguingly, an entry in a newsletter advertising the fair notes that one of the items displayed in the "Curiosity Shop" was "a piece of the bark of the Charter Oak." This relic almost certainly came from Church, who made three paintings of the famous Hartford, Connecticut, tree in the 1840s and acquired several branches and twigs, some of which were used to fashion an armchair that still sits in the library at Olana. Frederic and Isabel Church were both great music lovers, and while no record has yet surfaced of their attendance at a concert in Hudson Hall, they almost surely enjoyed performances there.

Hudson Hall remains a cultural mainstay in the city, hosting the annual

City Hall, left, and Warren Street, as Frederic Church would have known it. Photo courtesy Hudson Hall.

Hudson Jazz Festival, performances in classical music and the American songbook, a community chorus, and art exhibitions. It has also become, as the *New York Times* suggested in 2023, "a Baroque opera destination" and has earned widespread accolades for director R. B. Schlather's productions of George Frideric Handel's operas *Rodelinda* and *Giulio Cesare*. Both of these thrilling performances featured the period ensemble Ruckus, which *Times* reporter Joshua Barone praised for performing "opera with the spirit of a band from a music hall or dance party."

Niagara Falls

In 2022, in the large picnic area that embraces views of the Berkshires, Taconics, and Green Mountains, The Olana Partnership featured one of its more

Diana Wege's *Sacred Site* exhibition, with Becraft Mountain at right and Mount Merino at left.

unusual works of public art: *Sacred Site* by Diana Wege. The installation consisted of twelve huge paintings replicating—some precisely, some imaginatively—Frederic Church's influential 1867 *Niagara Falls, from the American Side*. Wege's intention was to raise awareness about the climatic and environmental challenges we face today.

Church made multiple trips to Niagara Falls and produced at least twenty-three studies. Amelia Sturges, a young diarist and art lover who was there during one of his visits in July 1856, left a colorful reminiscence of the painter. In a letter to her mother she wrote that Church, who had given her one of his sketches, "is intoxicated with Niagara. He rises at sunrise and we only see him at meal times. He is so restless away from the Falls that he cannot keep still, always feeling as if he were losing some new effect of light." Sturges described how while others relaxed in the evenings and listened to a band playing "delightful music," Church would excuse himself and say, "Well good night, I am going down to see the effect of moonlight and shadow."

Historian Barbara Babcock Millhouse describes how Church, in search of a unique aerial vantage point, climbed a tree at the falls, "hacked away obstructive foliage, and sketched as he balanced precariously on a limb." Church's *Niagara* was so vivid that John Ruskin, the famous English art critic, mistook the rainbow in the painting for a real one that he thought was reflected in a window of the London gallery where it was exhibited in 1857. Ruskin's error, Millhouse writes, "became widely known and enhanced Church's reputation for incontestable accuracy."

Frederick Law Olmsted led an international campaign to save Niagara Falls by persuading the State of New York to acquire and preserve the lands around it. In 1883 the state legislature passed a law establishing the Niagara Reservation, and Olmsted and his partner, Calvert Vaux, were hired to create a plan to preserve the scenic landscape, which in 1885 became the first state park in the nation.

But it was Frederic Church, intoxicated by the majesty of Niagara Falls, who had sounded an alarm about the rapid development of hotels and tourist attractions that were threatening the landscape around it. In 1879 Olmsted explained in a letter: "My attention was first called to the rapidly approaching ruin of its characteristic scenery by Mr. F. E. Church about ten years ago. Shortly afterwards, several gentlemen, frequenters of the Falls, met at my request, to consider this danger." It seems likely that Church had conveyed to Olmsted the same sentiments he shared in a letter to another friend in 1858: that "the cheap fares bring a great many queer people to the Falls," and "there is but a step from the sublime to the ridiculous" in the perception of "the Awful Cataract" and the persons who "swarm the Hotels." Church was one of the first to complain about the tourist hordes at Niagara Falls, and he did so in great style, admitting that the many "persons" he was forced to encounter pulled his attention away from contemplation of the falls "to the study of human character." His letter goes on: "I am somewhat annoyed too as they seem to think that the *quarter* which gives them admission to Goat Island also conveys the privilege of gaping over the shoulders of modest artists when engaged in studying the various effects of the Falls."

A century later it would be understood, as art historian John K. Howat writes in his seminal book *Frederic Church*, that "the restoration and salvation of Niagara Falls as a scenic marvel can properly be attributed to [Church], whose depictions of the site helped raise it to the status of international icon."

The Erratics

"Erratics" are what geologists call large, occasionally huge, rocks that were picked up by moving glaciers and transported far—sometimes hundreds of miles—from their original location. As the climate warmed the ice melted and water flowed away, but the boulders were left behind. Robert and Johanna Titus, who have been writing about the geology of the Hudson River Valley for decades, have found and examined erratics that appear to have been brought to this area from as far away as the Adirondacks in northern New York and the Green Mountains of Vermont.

Robert Titus and an erratic.

They are called "erratics," the Tituses explain, because they usually don't fit in with the local bedrock. They're wanderers, ancient relics of the ice age that sculpted and formed the Hudson Valley. They also happen to be excellent natural backrests for sitting on the ground and reading a book, picnicking, or just meditating in the landscape. (A recurring thought I have during my meditations in this spot is that if Frederic Church had been a pop star instead of the most famous painter of the day, he might have called his band FC and the Erratics). In a photo from one of his geology tours (at left), Robert Titus points to a particularly fine erratic on Ridge Road, wearing a T-shirt that reminds us: “No glaciers, no paintings.” He estimates this rock has been here for some fifteen thousand years.

Standing just outside the Ombra, a visitor gazes south toward the "Bend in the River" of Inbocht Bay.

SECTION 4: NEW APPROACH ROAD, 1887–1888

If you take a landscape tour of Olana in the twenty-first century, your donkey now replaced with a fully electric carriage, the approach to what Frederic Church called his "Feudal Castle" at the top of the hill is one of the most dramatic moments. For me, the most interesting thing about the spectacularly beautiful and singular manor house Church designed was his decision to essentially hide it in the landscape, so he could create pathways that would allow visitors to come upon it from different angles, offering them a frisson of joy in the discovery of this unique architectural gem that sits high on the hilltop. The house itself was never intended to be the focus of the views at Olana. There are places throughout the park where you catch a glimpse of it, or its intriguingly colorful parts—minarets, patterned chimneys, stonework, and gables—but for the most part Church designed his carriage roads, including the entrances to the property, in such a way that the house would forever be a surprise but not the main event.

New Approach Road is the only carriage road at Olana that doesn't bear the original name given it by Church, which we know from the 1886 *Plan of Olana*, but it was how the artist referred to the new drive when he wrote to his friend Erastus Dow Palmer in 1886 to say "I have laid out a new approach to the House." The name is a bit prosaic and not entirely historic, but it's how the Olana staff refers to it.

A Real-World Panorama

I had been coming to Olana for forty years before I truly saw the place in the way Church wanted me to. Kay's Carriage—named in honor of Kay Toll, a former board chair—was one of the first electric vehicles The Olana Partnership purchased. I was delighted to learn from Mark Prezorski that when they placed the first order for a Polaris GEM (for Global Electric Motorcar) the group opted for the white model, partly in tribute to the Syrian donkeys who first escorted guests and family members through this landscape in the 1870s. Every vehicle in the fleet is donkey white.

Whether you go by foot or electric vehicle up the New Approach Road, you'll be having the experience of Olana that Church designed for you. It also happens to be one of the most exciting, imaginative journeys you can take in an American landscape. The first time I made this excursion with Mark on a beautiful June day, I had the sensation of being in a real-world panorama—and I don't mean the kind you can make with your iPhone. In the era before photography, a different kind of "panorama craze" arrived in America from Europe, where it originated in the late eighteenth century. Those panoramas consisted of painted images that actually moved: long, rolled-up canvases that were unspooled before audiences in theaters. One popular example was Henry Lewis's 45,000-square-foot *Mammoth Panorama of the Mississippi River*, which opened in Kentucky theaters in 1849. You could get a seat in the dress circle or parquet for fifty cents. (A second-tier box went for a quarter.) "Doors opened at seven forty-five," historian Barbara Novak explains, "and the Panorama commenced moving at 8 ½ precisely." In effect it was, she notes, "a moving picture," a kinetic, almost cinematic, experience of a work of art.

The biggest of all was *The Grand Panorama of a Whaling Voyage 'Round the World* by Benjamin Russell and Caleb Purrington. Painted in 1848, the 1,275 feet of this exhibit was, according to the New Bedford Whaling Museum, "America's longest painting—longer than the Empire State Building is tall." The painting itself tells a story that gains in drama and tension as the scroll moves along, culminating with scenes of whaling ships tossed in the waves, their sails shortened, bobbing between icebergs as one boat goes down, nose first, into the sea. The panorama was exhibited in a huge picture frame that was bracketed by curtains; the audience sat facing the "stage" and watched in awe as narrative unfolded. Too fragile to be displayed as it was originally intended, the Whaling Museum has digitized the entire thing, and it's almost as thrilling to scroll through it, scene by scene, on the museum's website.

If that image looks familiar, it's because Church's most famous painting,

The Heart of the Andes, was exhibited in the same way: placed in a massive, windowlike frame and flanked on both sides by a capacious set of curtains that brought the scene center stage. Church surrounded the painting with tropical vegetation to evoke the South American landscape of the Andes, and the whole thing was lit by gas jets in what in what David Huntington described as a *mise en scène*. Painted just a decade after the whaling voyage panorama, this enormous painting was directly inspired by Church's great hero, naturalist and explorer Alexander Von Humboldt, who believed that panoramic paintings were ideally suited to depict the "essence" of the natural world.

Historian David Seamon summarizes Humboldt's philosophy by explaining that these "large-scale depictions of a region's unchanging qualities would provoke scientists to ask further questions about natural processes, which would lead to greater scientific understanding. In turn, this objective knowledge would lead artists to deeper intuitive insights about nature. The result would be a virtuous circle between art and science, each enhancing and furthering the other."

The Grand Panorama of a Whaling Voyage 'Round the World by Benjamin Russell and Caleb Purrington, 1848. Courtesy the New Bedford Whaling Museum.

When Church exhibited *Heart of the Andes* in 1859 it was received in the same spirit of excitement that the first moving panoramas had generated. All day long people stood in line to view the painting—so many the police were called to manage the crowd and keep the street clear. Inside, it was standing room only.

The painting showed Humboldtian details in the landscape: "a vast climatic range," as historian Kevin Avery described it, "the evolution of land forms from their volcanic origins" and the "movement of water itself from snowy mountain slope to icy stream to navigable river." It toured America and Britain and, like a theater or opera production, programs were available at the door

Frederic Edwin Church, *The Heart of the Andes*, as exhibited at the Metropolitan Fair in Aid of the Sanitary Commission, New York, 1864. Photographer unknown.

that unpacked every aspect of the creation: its geology, flora and fauna, and geography. Like many art lovers, Mark Twain visited the painting multiple times and brought opera glasses to better examine its features. He wrote to his brother that *Heart of the Andes* left his "brain gasping and straining with futile efforts to take all the wonder in."

I confess that my brain did a bit of gasping too, the first time I moved through the bends and curves of New Approach Road in Kay's Carriage. The first view we have is of "the Bend in the River," as Church called it, to the southwest; directly below is the Olana Lake, and, rising above it, Crown Hill; to the east we see the handsome form of Blue Hill rising, and behind that the low mountains of the Taconic Range. Driving up the hill, the road bends again, and part of the house comes into view—a minaret on one side, a tower on another—but only partially and for a moment before they're obscured by trees and the undulation of the hill. Now we're heading west, and on a winter day we can see, through the branches of the trees, the outlines of the Rip Van Winkle Bridge, the Catskill Mountains, and the Hudson River. Now we bend again to the north, and suddenly the entire house appears, its multiple textures, columns, and colors presenting as a kind of architectural gem. Barbara Novak called Church's polychromatic, fortress-like home "an Arabian Nights fantasy" for its Persian influence, but as I came to learn there are references to many international styles: from Mexico, Europe, South America, China, and Japan.

On the final approach to the house, a long, sinuous stone retaining wall draws our eye up the last bit of hill to the house. Beneath the wall is "mingled garden" that Isabel Church and her daughter, Downie, tended with great love.

The journey down the hill is just as dramatic, the panorama now experienced from a different seat in Frederic Church's outdoor theater. Every time I stroll along this road I think of something that great rambler Thomas Cole said: "How I have walked . . . day after day, and all alone, to see if there was not something among the old things which was new!" Cole's biographer Louis Legrand Noble observed that "such was the law to which his footsteps were ever patiently obedient; such was his way," and as he walked even well-known paths he did so "with the sweet wonder of a boy's first time."

This, for me, is the greatest joy of Olana: Every time I come here I see something new. The landscape is constantly changing as a result of the weather, the season, the time of day, and "the old things," as Cole put it, are always new again.

The Old Sign on Tenth Street by Edward Lamson Henry, 1877. Collection, National Academy of Design, New York, Gift of the Artist on election to membership. *The Old Sign on Tenth Street* was made by Edward Lamson Henry in February 1877. According to art historian Annette Blaugrund, there was a note attached to the back of the painting in which Henry identified the two figures walking past the Tenth Street Studio as William Beard and William de Haas, painters who each had a studio in the building, as did Henry himself. One of the figures carries a framed canvas under his arm; in the street, a prison van makes its way down Tenth Street to the courthouse.

It's a lovely evocation of old New York, and a street where I lived for twelve years that is still, according to Greenwich Village tour guides, haunted by the nattily dressed ghost of my great-great-grandfather, John LaFarge, who also had a studio in No. 51. When I reached out to the National Academy of Design to request permission to include the painting here, I learned it was intended to be displayed as part of a 1980 exhibition titled *Next to Nature: Landscape Paintings from the National Academy of Design* but was stolen just before the show opened. Thankfully a photograph had been included in the exhibition catalog, which was edited by Barbara Novak with text about E. L. Henry by Blaugrund. That photograph appears here.

Church's Studios

Unlike his teacher, who seems to have had little interest in city life, Frederic Church divided his time between New York and Hudson. In the city he worked at the famous Tenth Street Studio alongside such artists as Sanford Gifford, Winslow Homer, Jervis McEntee, Albert Bierstadt, Emanuel Leutze, and John LaFarge. The handsome building, between Fifth and Sixth Avenues (and torn down in the 1950s), was designed by Richard Morris Hunt. It was "an experiment," an 1858 article in *The Crayon* explained, "intended to provide studios for artists, accompanied with an exhibition-room." It was the first modern facility designed solely to serve the needs of artists, and Church was an inaugural tenant. He had a large studio on the second floor that was "softly lighted" and adorned with various trophies from his travels, including "an immense palm branch," a "monstrous buffalo's head," an armchair upholstered in the skin of a panther, and "a butterfly hung in a frame." He kept this studio until 1889.

In 1865, after several years of working out of a makeshift space on the farm, Church built a studio for himself at Olana, in a spot where he had hiked many times with Thomas Cole when he was a student. The location has a stunning view of the Olana lake, which Church designed to reflect the shape of the distant, wide Inbocht Bay in the Hudson River, and of course the Catskills under an ever-changing sky. At the time, this was the highest point on his property. The building is gone—Church himself dismantled it after he had completed the studio wing in his new house—and the original stone foundation is invisible, buried under the grass, but it's a very popular spot for *plein air* artists and students today. Archaeological explorations conducted in the 1990s unearthed items like glass medicine bottles, ceramics, and a paint tube that was identified as a very fine quality white lead paint. The excavation also uncovered enough pieces of window glass to suggest that the studio had windows on at least the north and west walls. In 1888, after inheriting almost half a million dollars from his father, Church began work on the studio wing on the north side of the house.

David Seamon explains that Church preferred to work in both environments, city and country, and "did not consider a work finished until he had seen it in the light of both studios." He worked in this studio on New Approach Road for twenty-three years.

The Bend in the River

Ten years after an epic battle stopped a massive electric power plant from being built on Storm King Mountain in the Hudson Highlands, a diverse group of "intervenors" a bit farther north in the Hudson Valley came together to stop an even larger behemoth: a 1,200-megawatt water-cooled nuclear power plant that the Power Authority of New York (PASNY) proposed to build in the tiny hamlet of Cementon. The site, on the west bank of the Hudson and around five miles south of Thomas Cole's house, had been named by Church "the Bend in the River." Formally known as Inbocht Bay, it is an area where the Hudson expands more than two miles into what Church described as "a lake-like sheet of water which is always dotted with steamers and other craft." Inbocht Bay became the centerpiece of Olana's viewscape, first from Church's studio on New Approach Road and later from the house he would build at the top of the hill.

PASNY (today's New York Power Authority) announced the project in 1973, and two years later the Nuclear Regulatory Commission recommend that it be approved. For decades this part of Greene County was home to the heavy industry of cement making—enough to name a town after it—and residents had become used to the endless parade of trucks going to and from loading docks, the ubiquitous cement dust that covered their cars and gardens, and puffs of smoke that had become a fixture of the landscape. But the PASNY plant was a totally new sort of creature: Its 450-foot stack would vent a plume of smoke that could be seen for miles. And that plume would rise straight up into a landscape that many consider the cradle of American art and culture.

The victory at Storm King marked the beginning of the modern environmental movement and led to the formation of Olana's great conservation partner, Scenic Hudson. Its most important legacy was to enshrine in law, for the first time ever, the right of ordinary citizens to bring environmental disputes to court; to have, in other words, constitutional standing in the protection of their own place. This is what enabled a large group of individuals and non-profit organizations to collectively fight, David-and-Goliath style, the State of New York and the powerful nuclear energy industry. Most remarkable was a surprise, and wildly improbable, intervenor who emerged toward the end of the long battle: a small oil painting from the hand of Frederic Edwin Church.

Like Storm King, the PASNY plant posed a significant environmental threat, but that's not what the intervenors focused on. Most heinous of all, they argued, was the *aesthetic* threat: the fatal blow that would be delivered upon this precious and historic viewscape. In essence, their argument was that the landscape mattered because in its broad, majestic, sweep it contained a vital American story, one of character, culture, industry, and art.

The PASNY case was noteworthy for the motley character of the intervenors who came together from both sides of the river to challenge the NRC's authorization to build the plant. Indispensable in the fight, and never fully acknowledged for her contribution, was Loretta Simon, an art teacher who fell in love with the landscape of the Hudson Valley after her husband gave her a book about the Catskill Mountain House. At around the same time the plant was announced a red-headed third grader in her class mentioned that his great-great-grandfather was a painter and volunteered that his mother would bring over one of his paintings for the class to examine. "I never forgot that moment," Simon told me years later, when this extremely generous young woman entered the class carrying "a detailed oil of an intimate size with a wide, ornate gold frame," painted by Thomas Cole. Over a period of seven years Simon schooled herself in the legal system and environmental law, raised money to support the efforts of the opposition groups, attended all the hearings in Albany, and became Greene County's representative in the fight against the plant.

Also essential in the battle was Winthrop Aldrich, assistant commissioner of the Department of Environmental Conservation and a tenth-generation member of one of America's oldest aristocratic families. Aldrich hired a Poughkeepsie lawyer, Robert Stover, and assembled an impressive group of expert witnesses who gave testimony in Albany, including Harvey K. Flad, a professor at Vassar whose scholarship focused on cultural and historic landscapes; Alan Gussow, an American landscape painter, writer, and environmental activist; and David Huntington, the former art student who had led the charge to save Olana from being sold in the 1960s. Four nonprofits joined the group of intervenors: the Hudson River Conservation Society; Columbia County Historical Society; Citizens to Preserve the Hudson Valley; and the Friends of Olana, today The Olana Partnership.

Carl Petrich was an environmental scientist at Oak Ridge, one of several national laboratories used by the United States Department of Energy to evaluate nuclear power plants. Having a background in landscape architecture, he was given the task of drafting an Environmental Impact Statement for the Nuclear Regulatory Commission, which they were required by law to publish, along with instituting a public comment period, before granting a license. Petrich, who grew up in Ohio, knew nothing of Frederic Church and the Hudson River School, so he consulted "the Google of the time," *The Reader's Guide to*

View from Olana with superimposed simulated nuclear cooling towers. Photograph #4363-77, Courtesy of Oak Ridge National Laboratory, US Department of Energy, 1979.

Periodical Literature, where he found a long article on Olana that had been published in *Life* magazine in 1966. He sought out David Huntington for insight into the importance of Church's home and studied the work of Rachel and Stephen Kaplan, Berkely social scientists who had developed a functional approach to landscape aesthetics through preference surveys that enabled a deeper, and science-based, understanding of how people feel about their environment and why landscape matters. He consulted art historians who were experts on Church's work, including John Wilmerding and Barbara Novak.

At the time, the idea of using an aesthetic argument to fight a power plant was considered unorthodox at best. When I interviewed Wint Aldrich in 2013, he recalled that the major players in the Storm King battle urged the PASNY intervenors to change their focus. "Pete Seeger's people told us 'you can't win on aesthetics,'" Aldrich told me. "They felt what we were doing was ridiculous and frivolous . . . that we were making this silly old lady's argument about the view," when the real issue had to do with how energy was being used and the impact on fish. "We were told we had to base an argument on *environmental issues* and the question of need: did there *need* to be a plant here—otherwise we were doomed to failure."

But the group continued to keep its focus on the primacy of the place and its views. A key moment in the battle occurred when David Huntington traveled to Albany and submitted, along with his testimony as an expert witness, a copy of a work by Frederic Church of Olana in winter. The centerpiece of the small oil painting is the "Bend in the River" in Inbocht Bay. Because the original painting was, at that very moment, hanging on display in Albany's New York State Museum in an exhibit devoted to the Hudson River School, the entire panel of administrative judges who were hearing the case left the courtroom and walked over to the museum to see it for themselves. It was, Loretta Simon told me, "the crowning touch in discrediting the PASNY opinion that the plant could be sited in Cementon."

In the end, Petrich's research definitively concluded, as he stated in the report on behalf of the Nuclear Regulatory Commission, that "building the power plant in [Cementon] would entail an unacceptable, negative aesthetic impact," and recommended the license be denied. The judges who had heard the long case agreed and based their ruling to deny a construction permit in aesthetic reasons: because the plume of smoke from the plant's 450-foot stack would mar the view from Olana.

Thus it was that a small—only around 8 ½" × 13"—painting became the powerful monolith that stopped a nuclear power plant. It's thought to be the first time in American history that a landscape painting was used as the defining force in a legal proceeding, when both the beauty of the view and its cultural value would predominate over more traditional issues in conservation battles like the protection of species, habitats, or quality of air and water. It was also the first—and so far the only—time the Nuclear Regulatory Commission has denied a construction license on grounds related to aesthetic impact. Visitors on house tours at Olana can admire this lovely painting for themselves, since it hangs in the corridor that leads to Church's studio—a spot that offers a particularly grand view down Inbocht Bay.

Looking back on the fight some thirty years later, Rick Benas, a land use expert who worked for the Department of Environmental Conservation and was a witness in the case, noted that giving testimony in the Olana suit was the first time in his career as a licensed landscape architect that "my professional opinion did not matter" in the question of aesthetics. Instead, he told me, it was "the collective wisdom of us all that spoke of the values of specially designated places" and new precedents in federal and state law that ended up determining aesthetic value. "The democratic political process, in essence, has established this discipline."

Another decade later, in 2024, Olana's Mark Prezorski summarized for me the entire affair in just three words: "People preserve places." If there is an abiding message at Olana, this is it.

The Olana House

On a bitter cold, lightly snowing December afternoon, Sean Sawyer, president of The Olana Partnership, met me for a conversation about Church's castle on the hill. In keeping with my focus on the landscape at Olana, it was Sean's idea to present the house entirely from the outside; to treat it, as Church did, as part of the larger place. As we ambled up the gentle, winding path he offered a thought to frame our visit: "We're walking here today in a *luftmeer*," he said, introducing Church's hero, Alexander von Humboldt, right as the journey started. Translated literally it means "air ocean" or "sea of air," and it was Humboldt's poetic way of describing Earth's atmosphere in a way that captured the vast, interconnected world of nature.

In her marvelous biography *The Invention of Nature*, Andrea Wulf writes that Humboldt stored the "ever increasing flood of knowledge" he gleaned from newspaper cuttings, letters, pages from books, drawings, notes, and "long tables of temperatures," in boxes and envelopes that he sorted by category. There were notes about crocodiles and elephants found in Hebrew poetry, slavery, meteorology, astronomy, and botany. Quoting a fellow scientist, Wulf emphasizes that "no one but Humboldt could so dexterously tie together so many 'loose ends' of scientific research into one beautiful knot." This is a thought worth keeping front of mind as you approach Frederic Church's singular home. Inspired by Humboldt, Church was a close, enthusiastic observer of nature's drama, to the point where it sometimes interfered with his work. In 1870 he shared this complaint with a friend in a letter, telling him that "splendid Meteoric displays" were interrupting his "usual steady devotion" to his work on the new house. When he created a beautiful sketch of the house two years later he made the sky and atmosphere the main event, placing the dwelling in darkness below a wide swath of cumulonimbus clouds that hover under a patch of blue sky.

So when you go, be sure to observe the weather.

When you first see the house at Olana, it will quite possibly leave you speechless. Influenced by Moorish and Middle Eastern motifs that Church found, and fell in love with, in large-format, lavishly illustrated books of historical monuments like shrines, mosques, and palatial complexes he purchased after an eighteen-month long trip to Europe and the Middle East, the house is an awe-inspiring mix of textures, colors, and shapes, made from a wide array of materials: different types of stone, colored bricks, ceramic tile, and wood. Further delighting the eye are stunning, hand-stenciled ornamentations on the exterior cornices that Church himself designed. At least twenty different colors were used in the stencils, including gold and silver metallic finishes Church created by adding powdered aluminum and bronze to paints—now sadly faded away—and they decorate the different sections of a magnificent house that rises on the hill in a collection towers, porches, balconies, arched windows—some of which are bordered with amber glass—and mansard roofs. Even The Olana Partnership, on its richly comprehensive website, concedes that the house "is difficult to categorize."

In a case like this it's always wise defer to a poet. John Ashbery, who lived in Hudson for almost forty years, wrote that "the ensemble is breathtaking, and despite the proliferation of architectural elements and polychrome tile decoration, it is not busy but solemn and wildly fanciful, like Church's painting. . . . It is as though a moral and aesthetic lesson (on the order of Hopkins' line 'The world is charged with the grandeur of God') was being wordlessly expounded."

One of the first elements Sean Sawyer drew my eye to is the patterning in the stone walls: different shapes, colors, and textures, some running horizontally along the façade in small, loopy sections that look like pieces in a jigsaw puzzle, and some in more formal geometric patterns. "My understanding from the *Historic Structures Report*," he observed, "is that much as it looks like a stone house, it's actually a brick house." That beautiful, artistic puzzle of stone is, in fact, a veneer that Frederic Church applied to a brick façade, since the softer sandstone wouldn't hold up a structure as large as the house he was planning to build. It's as though he used brick as a canvas and then turned the exterior of the house into one large work of art, using stone for decoration instead of paint. Interlaced through the improvisationally strewn sandstone patterns are pieces of bluestone, cut into squares and rectangles, and higher up are bricks in different colors that Church arranged in patterns that seem, to Sawyer's eye, "almost postmodern." The overall effect is one of playfulness, exotic in its presentation, utterly original and, as the poet said, breathtaking.

It fascinated me to learn from Sawyer that all this stone was locally sourced, blasted from the hilltop at Olana or purchased from stoneworks in Ulster County, just across the river, and brickyards in Stockport and Albany. Church had the money to design like a Livingston; he could have imported the best

The Olana castle as a visitor arrives on New Approach Road.

stones from Alabama, where quarries were renowned for rocks that resembled Carrara marble, but he favored materials that came from the Hudson Valley. True to the vision of the man who created it, the house is built from the landscape itself.

Church had no background in architecture, and he turned to Calvert Vaux for valuable assistance with the mechanics of construction, the massing of the building and how to handle three-dimensional relationships. Vaux, whose personal credo was "Nature first, second, and third—architecture after a while," was a kindred spirit, a fellow artist Church knew he could trust with this most personal and monolithic project.

The design of the house, constructed between 1870 and 1874 at the top of what was then called Sienghenbergh, or Long Hill, unfolded in a close collaboration between both Churches, Frederic and Isabel. After their long trip overseas in 1867–1869, during which they spent five months in Beirut, the Churches came home to Hudson filled with ideas for their new home. Some nineteenth-century visitors saw, and recorded, the hand of Isabel Church in the creation of Olana, among them the biologist and botanical artist Marianne North, who recorded in her diary that it was Isabel who "contrived to make the whole collection of curiosities look like the natural parts of a comfortable living-house." Isabel's daughter, Downie, wrote to her father's biographer, Charles Dudley Warner, in 1899 asking: "*Could* my little Mother's great part in Papa's life, her influence on his building this house too be brought in? . . . I have not mentioned this to Papa—but he has often spoken of how *her* taste in the house is shown from top to bottom—and her advice was asked about it all."

Only in recent years have scholars begun to acknowledge the role of Isabel Church in designing the house. Karen Zukowski, a historian who has contributed important research in this area, credits Isabel with having a hand in "transforming the hardscrabble hill" at Olana into a farm and in the siting and design of the house, for being Frederic's "consultant in all matters of design and furnishing," and for translating from the French Pascal Coste's *Monuments moderns de la Perse*, one of the principle sources Church used for his stencils. Perhaps most consequential to a modern visitor, it was Isabel who came up with the name for the house, having learned about a Persian fortress named Olana.

What surprised the environmental scientist Carl Petrich when he finally visited Olana is *what we cannot see*. "There are details that nobody would see but the artist himself or his family," Petrich discovered, "and they took an excruciating amount of time to do things, like up on the roof: there's things that you'd never see from the ground, and they just did it for themselves."

When I first had the great joy of climbing up the attic stairs to the belltower, I understood what Petrich meant: Here, in an open air room with Middle Eastern–style brick arches and a genuinely sublime—this is the only time in this book I'll use that word—view of the Hudson Valley landscape, are elements we *don't* see from the ground below: multicolored patterns in stone, brick, and tile that adorn the lower parts of chimneys, towers, and roof gables. I had never fully appreciated the circular black and gold design that decorates the rounded section at the bottom of the minaret above Church's new studio. And it was exciting to get close enough to touch the two-hundred-pound bell the Churches brought home from Mexico.

Even higher than the bell tower is the Crow's Nest, which presents a 360-degree view of the entire region through brick arches and is crowned at each corner with a Japanese teapot, which Church used as finials. Early one

Christmas morning I walked up the hill to discover an enormous black bird perched on the decorative railing, gazing south toward the famous view of Inbocht Bay. It wasn't a crow, though; zooming in through my telephoto lens, I could tell it was a black vulture who was eyeing the Bend in the River.

Beneath the vulture are more stencils and little ceramic figures that sit inside small arched openings. On the south-facing façade is a balcony with a series of columns that has lovely Middle Eastern–looking capitals sourced from one of Church's pattern books; this was the children's nursery, which included indoor and outdoor environments and multiple doors for easy, fluid access.

Facing south, toward the Bend in the River, is a large, deep-set veranda known as the Ombra. This a word Vaux first used in the early 1860s when he was designing the Moses Sheppard Asylum in Maryland, a state institution for people suffering from mental illness. The Ombra was the place where patients could enjoy fresh air, a central tenet in Sheppard's philosophy about providing humane care to the mentally ill. Olana's Ombra was the place where the family gathered, relaxed, read, or snoozed in a large wicker lounge nicknamed "Grasshopper."

"They are always looking out the windows," a close friend of Isabel Church's, Susan Hale, remembered, and the importance of views, fresh air, and light is

A vulture admires the view down Inbocht Bay, perched on the railing of the Crow's Nest between two Japanese teapots.

manifest everywhere at the Olana house, including in the servant's quarters. Pointing up to the windows above the former service entrance—now used by staffers at The Olana Partnership and New York State Parks—Sawyer commented on how the household staff were also windows onto the landscape as well.

Countless writers have tried to capture in words the magic of this place, but it seems it was always an impossible project. Church himself couldn't do it. "You notice that I write in an absent minded sort of way," he said to a friend in a letter, "crossing out and inserting words; well it is owing to the magnificent effects this morning—beautiful clouds, an opalescent atmosphere, and lovely tints in the landscape distract me every minute."

Fallen Hemlock

In 2021 Olana exhibited a deeply moving installation called *Fallen* by artist Jean Shin. A beloved hemlock (*Tsuga canadensis*) that had stood sentinel on the East Lawn of the Olana hilltop for 140 years died of natural causes. Shin is an artist known for using cast-off and scavenged materials—items like Mountain Dew bottles, 35mm slides, and mobile phones—as a way of focusing attention on everyday objects and shining a light on modern society's hunger for material consumption and its consequences. For *Fallen*, she used tools that were employed by the nineteenth century tanning industry to "ceremoniously" peel back the bark of the forty-foot dead tree trunk and transform it into a colorful, leather-clad monument that rested on two large boulders outside the front door of the house. When staffers from NYS Parks counted the rings on the stump, they learned that this hemlock was approximately the same age as Church's house, dating to around the early 1870s.

Hemlocks were killed by the millions in the early nineteenth century because the tanning industry relied on tannin in the tree's bark for leathermaking. To make a connection between the wastefulness of the fashion business and the fragility of our natural ecosystems, Shin used discarded leather offcuts from industry giants like Marc Jacobs and Chloé and attached them to dead wood with brass upholstery tacks. She explained to the *New York Times* that it created for the tree an "armor-like . . . protection, a defense against further injury." The hemlock's stump still remains in the woods near the house.

Fallen was part of a larger mapping project at Olana that identified more than five hundred eastern hemlocks throughout the landscape. Jean Shin created leather tags adorned with lovely engraved sketches of the hemlock's needles; these were hung from tree branches along the various carriage roads and remained in place throughout the exhibition season. When a gust of wind came through the forest, they twirled and floated in the breeze. The tags were also part of a survey of remaining hemlocks the custodians of Olana were conducting throughout the park and were an unmissable reminder of both of the historic presence of these beautiful trees in the landscape and also of a new threat they face, posed by an aphid-like insect called the woolly adelgid (*Adelges tsugae*). Native to Asia, this tiny creature feeds on the sap at the base of hemlock needles, disrupting the flow of nutrients and severely damaging the tree's canopy. As the amount of photosynthesis is reduced by the loss of its needles, the tree will eventually die. By "making visible the layers of history, loss, and rebirth in this landscape," Shin wrote on her web-

Jean Shin, *Fallen Hemlock*, on Olana's south lawn, May 2021.

site, "the artist invites visitors to observe the hemlock's beauty while urging us to consider how the absence of this still-threatened species would impact the ecosystem."

The Mingled Garden

Following the curve of the handsome retaining wall just below the house is a garden that was laid out in the 1880s as a colorful feature to greet people just as they made the final approach to the home. Original invoices from Church's nurseryman tell us the garden was filled with a great variety of different plant types, with common names including pansies, chrysanthemum, sweet alyssum, calceolaria, centaurea, calendula, heliotrope, vinca, coleus, echeveria, salvia, aster, anthemis, lemon verbena, lobelia, begonia, geranium, rose geranium, verbena, yellow lantana, nasturtium, zinnia, columbine, blue ageratum, marigold, Japanese poppy, pale yellow columbine, dahlias, salpiglossis, and Japanese corona. There were vine plants too, which suggest the garden was conceived for both its horizontal and vertical planes: cobea, maurandia, nasturtium, and clematis.

The concept of a "mingled garden" at Olana is another example of the influence of Andrew Jackson Downing, who used the phrase to express his love of variety in a garden: the blending of different species of plants to create a picturesque scene outside a home. In his treatise on landscape gardening, Downing explained that the purpose of "the *mingled* flower-garden . . . is to dispose the plants in the beds in such a manner that, while there is no predominance of bloom in any one portion of the beds, there shall be a general admixture of colours and blossoms throughout the entire garden during the whole season of growth." Anyone who has visited the High Line park in New York City will recognize Downing's legacy here too, in the work of Piet Oudolf, whose signature garden design consists of combining the greatest variety of perennials, annuals, evergreens, shrubs, and deciduous trees to create a garden that presents an ever-changing, always intriguing palette of colors, textures, and aromas throughout the course of the year, from the height of summer to the frigid, windy days of winter.

In a letter to her daughter in July 1890, Isabel Church refers to "your garden." Downie, a supremely talented botanical artist, was deeply interested in the color, texture, and architectural form of plants, and it's likely that the mingled garden benefited from her artistic eye and sensibility. Her illustrations and paintings are beautiful, expressive, evocations of the lives of these plants, many of which she tended in her own "mingled garden," just below the house where she grew up.

The Mingled Garden was abandoned after Frederic Church's death, when Louis and Sally established a more formal garden on what is now the East Lawn. Research and restoration of the original garden began in the 1970s, through the combined efforts of the Friends of Olana staff and volunteers, and culminated in 2015. Today the garden is filled with flowering perennials and annuals, many of which attract bees, butterflies, hummingbirds, and other pollinators.

Olana Lake, at left, echoing the outlines of Inbocht Bay, at right.

SECTION 5: LAKE ROAD, 1884–1885

Frederic Church enthusiastically embraced the new field of landscape architecture. In his library was an 1853 book on the subject by Charles H. J. Smith, which pronounces: "Of the varied material in the composition of natural scenery, there is none that produces more beauty, variety and interest than water." Thomas Cole also revered the majesty of water in a landscape; in his *Essay on American Scenery* he wrote that a body of water "contributes greatly to the beauty of landscape; for the reflections of surrounding objects, trees, mountains, sky, are most perfect in the clearest water; and the most perfect is the most beautiful." The circular path of Lake Road traverses a thick forest and the road gently winds around the lake. No matter the weather—under a blue summer sky or entirely iced over in winter—the trees along the shoreline are reflected in the lake, a timeless phenomenon that must have made Church think happily of his teacher, Cole, whose words, ideas, and artistic values he took so much to heart.

Likely you will begin your walk Lake Road just outside the Frederic Church Center for Art and Landscape, at the top of the steps that lead up a small hill from the pavilion and amphitheater. Turning toward the lake, you'll be presented with one of Church's richest composed views. This is one of the few places where he puts his home at the center of the scene, framing it with trees on both sides that encircle the large lake. Below the house, opposite the lake, is a long, wide, park-like meadow; it's not a smooth hill but a terrain that has an undulating quality, rolling and dipping, an irregularity that adds to its beauty. Here is a place where the artist/architect has turned his eye on the natural forms and features of his landscape and invited a visitor who is moving through it to pause for just a moment to perceive *this* composition, before continuing on.

The terrain of Lake Road is different from all the others: It rises and falls, rather than proceeding in a constant upward or downward direction, as it winds around the curves of the shoreline. This pleasure drive differs in another interesting way: It's the only one where history records the hand of a woman in the design. In July

1884 Emma Carnes, Church's mother-in-law, recorded in her diary that "Mr. C. & Miss Hale marked out the road around the pond." Susan Hale was a prolific writer, traveler, lecturer, and watercolorist who was a traveling companion and great friend of Isabel Church. Much of her literary work and lecturing were aimed at educating women. Hale's 1885 book *Self-Instructive Lessons in Painting* offered practical, step-by-step instructions that would enable women of all ages to advance in the arts, beginning with "very pretty and attractive gifts and ornaments, based upon good principles of art and taste." Gradually, Hale promises in her introduction, the beginning artist would "find herself growing more and more capable of more difficult, more elaborate, and more individual work." Hale was an energetic, witty, athletic presence during her visits to Olana. At the time when they were "marking out the road" together, Hale recalled that Church, now suffering from rheumatoid arthritis, was "very stiff and lame, but lovely." It's an intriguing scene to imagine: these two very different artists, both well-traveled and omnivorous in their interests, wandering through the woods together and filling it with conversation as they marked, measured, and planned the many views and surprises along this new, extravagantly beautiful pleasure drive.

Olana Lake

Church spent close to twenty years dredging an old swamp on the property—"getting out muck," as Theodore Cole, son of Thomas and Church's farm manager, put it – and, as a budding farmer who was committed to an early form of composting, he then spread it over his farmland to improve the soil. It was a lot of muck, more formally known as peat, reportedly 40,000 cubic feet, which, according to the artist, entailed "not less than 5,000,000 loads." Perhaps an overstatement, but he valued his swamp soil very highly. "My muck seems wonderfully adapted to trees and I give them liberal doses of it," he wrote in an 1864 letter. But Church was also a savvy businessman, and in exchange for their labor he traded half of his precious, nutrient-rich muck with the local workmen who helped hand-dig the lake.

If you stand on the spot where he located his first studio, halfway up Long Hill with your back to the house and facing the lake, you will be able to discern one of the most striking of Church's composed views. Here, looking down the meadow, you can see how the artist designed the lake—how he guided all those laborers in their digging and muck-shoveling—to echo the contours of the "Bend in the River" some three miles to the southwest in Inbocht Bay, where the Hudson widens into a large, lake-like field. This spot, I think, is the very best place to appreciate the genius of Frederic Church's artistry, rendered not on a canvas in oils but in the landscape itself. Here he borrowed one piece of the existing scenery, the Hudson River, and created a new feature, a small lake, that would work together to form a completely natural, harmonic composition.

Church may have designed his lake as a scenic feature, but it was used by the family for many purposes: fishing and boating in summer, ice skating in winter, and bird watching throughout the year. The lake was also a great benefit to biodiversity, particularly beneficial to pollinators, who contributed to the health and success of the orchards and other crops. It was also the family's reservoir in the warm months, and a source of ice that was used year-round and stored in an icehouse near nearby. If you're lucky, you'll catch a fish jumping or a heron gliding into a landing on the surface of the water. There are also tortoises, a multitude of frogs, ducks, and very often a happy dog bounding into the water to retrieve a tennis ball before emerging in a fine suit of muck.

A woman meditates on the east shore of the Olana Lake.

The Business of Ice

In 1869 Frederic Church built an icehouse near the lake. Ice harvesting was a big business along the Hudson River, and in the nineteenth century, before houses had electricity, it was ice from lakes, ponds and rivers that kept food fresh. Church's icehouse was a roomy, wooden structure that would have been filled with blocks of ice that were insulated with straw or sawdust. According to members of the June family, who lived in Cosy Cottage in the early twentieth century when Louis and Sally

Church were in residence in the main house, the annual ice harvest at Olana took place each February. It took three days and required a large crew of workers who came from the Livingston farm nearby and stayed at Olana until the icehouse was full.

The harvesting, storage, and shipping of ice was one of first and the most important economic activities on the Hudson River in Church's time. There is a relic of the ice industry in Olana's viewshed, visible from Ridge Road: If you look to the north from the picnic area you'll see a handsome brick chimney standing along the edge of the river, in the town of Athens. Once a factory owned by the Knickerbocker Ice Company, this is one of the last remaining vestiges of a Hudson Valley industry that provided tens of thousands of pounds of ice each year to New York City.

Today all that is left of Olana's icehouse is a stone foundation near Lake Road, which gave easy access to the horse or donkey-drawn carts that would transport it from the lake.

Cosy Cottage

While their farm cottage was being built, the newlyweds Frederic and Isabel (Carnes) Church camped out at Cedar Grove, then the home of Theodore Cole, whose father had died in 1847 at the age of forty-seven. Church had sold *Heart of the Andes* for $10,000 in 1859—then the highest price ever paid for a painting by a living American artist—and he used every penny of that money to purchase 126 acres of land that had been farmed by a man named Wynsant Brezie. At the time, seventy acres were devoted to the harvesting of grain, and the rest supported a farmhouse, orchards, farm buildings and a woodlot. Now a wealthy, celebrated artist, he decided to begin his family in a rural idyll 120 miles north of his studio on Tenth Street in New York City.

The approach drive to the little house, which was designed in a then-popular ornamental style known as Cottages Ornées, was lined with sugar maples, and the cottage sits comfortably in the center of the bustling farm, perched over vast orchard fields. An 1867 newspaper article described the cottage as being in "the Gothic style" and "nestled in a vale, where the stretch of interior landscape reminds one of Devonshire, England." There was a three-acre kitchen garden in a fenced area nearby that provided the household with cut flowers, fruit, berries, vegetables, and other crops, and just outside the house were a hammock and "an elaborate bird feeder" designed as a kind of Swiss chalet. The lake nearby provided irrigation for the kitchen garden. Church was especially proud of his "Mexican corn," which grew as high as sixteen feet, prompting him to note that "my gardener measures but 5 feet and knocks off the ears with a club."

The architect Richard Morris Hunt provided design input into Cosy Cottage, but the spirit of the house is more informed by the ideas of Calvert Vaux and Andrew Jackson Downing, who both wrote influential books about American residential architecture in the context of landscape design. When I did a circumnavigation of the house with Sean Sawyer of The Olana Partnership, he noted that many of the design features were "gestures to make the building settle into the landscape." This type of ornamental cottage was "the big reaction that Downing and Vaux introduced in American rural design," he continued, moving far away from the ostentatious, colonnaded, bright white, Greek Revival homes that had been so popular. "Simplicity" was the ideal, Downing wrote; it should be the "predominant character" of a country house.

Cosy Cottage.

One important element in the creation of a cottage's character was color. In *The Architecture of Country Homes,* Downing wrote: "We think, in the beginning, that the color of all buildings in the country should be of those *soft and quiet shades,*" and the first one he listed was "fawn." Paint scrapings done during restoration of the cottage reveal that the lovely, mellow yellow of Cosy Cottage is indeed fawn. For anyone wanting to create this paint color for themselves, Downing left a helpful list of ingredients on page 187 of his book: "take 4 lbs. umber, 1 lb. Indian red, and 1/2 lb. lampblack . . ."

The Churches moved into the cottage in the spring of 1861 and lived there until the main house at the top of the hill was complete enough for the family to move into the upper floors in late summer 1872; it then became home to the farmer who helped manage the property and his family. Today, The Olana Partnership's administrative and curatorial staff have offices in Cosy Cottage.

The Preservation of Olana

The Olana Partnership emerged from what it calls a "miraculous preservation victory" in the 1960s as a nonprofit steward dedicated to preserving and interpreting this singular, extraordinary place: the artist-designed landscape; the house, including its physical structure, interiors, and collection; the carriage roads; Cosy Cottage, the farm and related buildings; and, of course, the viewshed.

I began coming to Olana in 1985. Just as I was finishing work on this book my sister Louisa sent me a photo she discovered in an old box of family papers. Dated June 1987, it shows my father, W. E. R. LaFarge, and me standing just below the house on what has come to be known as Church Hill. My dad, a poet and respected land and watershed conservationist in Rhode Island, was himself a gentleman farmer like Frederic Church. He understood and deeply appreciated the spirit of this place: an artist-designed landscape that was intended to be worked as a farm; journeyed on foot with friends in long walks that would present a series of delightful and surprising views; and create a home for a large family. I remember him saying "this is the most romantic place in the world."

Since that beautiful summer day forty years ago, an enormous amount of work has been undertaken by The Olana Partnership and NYS Parks. The stone façade on the house has been repointed, and research into the original stencils, wallpaper, and furnishings inside has enabled the group to do faithful conservation and reinstallation of historic decorative objects. In the landscape and farm complex, meadows, lake, and all the carriage roads have been restored to the condition the Church family would have known, including panoramic vistas that had been lost to second-growth vegetation. In addition to that work, several thousand acres in the Olana viewshed have been preserved, thanks to the efforts of numerous organizations and private landowners, some of whom open their scenic landscapes and working farms to the popular "Viewshed Tours" that take place each year.

Perhaps the most important thing to consider about the early efforts to save Olana is that the preservation principles established in the 1960s created a kind of roadmap for the future, both inspiring and informing campaigns to protect the viewshed from massive industrial projects like the planned nuclear power plant across the river in Greene County, and North America's largest cement factory just outside the city of Hudson. There were other battles too: one against a communications tower on Blue Hill, a handsome earth form that Frederic Church painted, and another effort to successfully alter height of the smokestacks and the color of the entire facility at the Athens Generating Plant in view from Ridge Road. More fights over the viewshed will almost certainly come in the future, and The Olana Partnership and its members and supporters have dedicated themselves to challenge any further intrusions on the historic landscape.

Another aspect of the organization's preservation work was the development of a wide range of activities at Olana, from events featuring food, gardening, *plein air* painting, and music to kite festivals, bird walks, artmaking and dance workshops. Sadly, the public is not invited to use the hills and lake as the Church kids did, for sledding, tobogganing, and skating, but in December you can come to the Olana solstice festival and meet Hank, a snow-white donkey who hangs out on the lawn just outside the house and carries on the long tradition that launched "a Donkey Fever" at Olana in 1869.

The Athens Generating Plant from Ridge Road.

Farm Road

In 1878, when Frederic Church decided he needed more pasture land, he purchased fifty acres of meadow just behind Cosy Cottage. The short road that intersects with North Road after about a quarter of a mile appears on the 1886 *Plan of Olana* as Farm Road, which was completed in 1869; this is where a parade of animals would have been herded past the cottage on their way to and from the barn to the open fields that were fenced off for hay production and grazing. Below the cottage, in the orchard fields, is the foundation and remains of the original Wynsant Brezie farmhouse.

As you look to the east on Farm Road you see an expansive meadow that is bracketed on three sides by the forest. In the years after Louis and Sally Church died this land was overtaken by second growth trees and invasives. In 2014 the meadow was restored with native grasses and perimeter plantings, and today it looks much as it did in the years when the property was a working farm. Looking west as you walk along Farm Road is a totally different scene: a rocky, glaciated hill that rises up, through the trees, to the top of Long Hill. The juxtaposition of meadow and forest makes this one of the most magical spots in Olana.

Frederic Church was, in the words of historian David Seamon, "a practical Yankee" who insisted that the farm pay for itself, so he planted crops that could easily be sold, which included fruits like pears, peaches, grapes, cherries, strawberries, raspberries, currants, plums, and apples along with feed crops like hay, rye, corn, and oats. Seamon adds that while Church was committed to developing and taking his cash crops to market, he also "made aesthetic use of the farmstead, manipulating the views of pastures, fields, and orchards." Olana was a residential farm, but also something more: "an expression of an ideal . . . the quest for beauty focused on landscape design practiced as a fine art."

There were animals everywhere: horses (stabled in a large barn near Cosy Cottage), pigs, geese, cows, oxen, turkeys, even peacocks. Church's young son Herbert would feed the chickens out of his hand, and they also had a pair of pigeons. From an early age Church was "a serious botanizer" who collected seeds from all over the world. In his letters he writes about "heavenly" morning glories he gathered in Mexico, "enchanting" roadside flowers in Bogotá, and melon seeds from Persia.

It was never a great moneymaker, but Church wrote in 1868 that "the farm pays," and he found this "very soothing." By the 1870s production had declined, and much of the property that had been used for fields was left unplowed, a development that pleased the artist because it enhanced the scenic quality of the land. A plowed lawn, he once said, "spoils the beauty of the scene somewhat." By 1875 he had reduced the amount of plowed land from more than sixty acres to less than twenty, which he used for the cultivation of oats, corn, and potatoes. According to Mark Prezorski, there is still a question of whether Church was moving away from farming or if he was, instead, inclining toward large-scale landscape and park design, which he would have observed firsthand as a recently appointed commissioner of Central Park.

When the Future Came to the Olana Farm

Louis Church wasn't as interested in farming as his father was, but like his older brother Frederic Joseph, he was intrigued by new technology. He loved ma-

Olana's historic farm buildings as seen from the top of Crown Hill.

chines, especially the automobile, which went into mass production in the late 1890s. Just after the turn of the century Louis remodeled his father's stable, reducing the space for horses so there would be room to park his "Glorious Motor Car," as Susan Hale referred to it, adding that "Louis is cracked about it." More technically, it was a "steam car," an early type of automobile that was powered by a steam engine instead of gasoline and was popular before the internal combustion engine predominated. That new technology also intrigued Louis, who by 1922, when he bought a Ford tractor, could plow his fields with a machine instead of the horses and oxen his father used.

Dogs of Olana

Dogs have a long, happy, history at Olana. I'm willing to bet Frederic Church was a big dog lover; all the evidence one needs is right there in his beautiful oil sketch of Oosisoak, a sled dog who accompanied his friend and student Isaac Hayes on an Arctic expedition in 1860. Historian Eleonor Jones Harvey writes that Church's painting "mimics the format and palette of so many of the portraits made of British Arctic explorers, shown frontally, dressed in their furs, against an icy backdrop." But what kills you are the dog's eyes, which focus intently on the viewer with deep seriousness and nobility; it's as if Church's purpose was to reveal the soul of this animal. In a letter to Hayes, Church confessed "it is my first attempt at animal painting and done too within two hours." The portrait of Oosisoak was a favorite of Isabel Church, and one of the few works her husband mentioned by name in his will.

Frederic Edwin Church, *Oosisoak*. Photo by David C. Huntington.

The Church family had several dogs over the years, and from letters and diary entries it is clear they were important members of the household. Frederic Joseph, the Churches' eldest son, had a dog named Boz in the 1860s (Isabel's mother, Mrs. Carnes, enthusiastically records in her diary that "Freddies dog arrived by express!") and Louis, the youngest, had Boca, whose bark was apparently quite impressive. Church's sense of humor comes out when he writes about dogs; in an 1876 letter he joked about how the bark of a cherry tree is "good for bow wowel complaints," then concluded with a tidbit about the talented Boca: "My dog would bark at your (and my) puns."

Olana has a dedicated section on its website for the Dogs of Olana and their humans, and you'll find them everywhere in the park.

The view from Crown Hill, with the farm in the foreground and the house peeking up through trees in the distance.

SECTION 6: CROWN HILL ROAD, 1884–1885

Church's mother-in-law, Emma Carnes, wryly commented to her diary in August 1885 that "Mr C is making another drive, thinks it's a secret!" (Offering, it's worth pointing out, historical evidence that it has *never* been possible to hide one's intentions from a mother-in-law.) The top of Crown Hill presents one of the most dramatic of Church's composed views, a panorama that takes in the Persian-inspired castle on the opposite hill, the carefully landscaped park below it, the lake, the farm and its barns, and the mountain ranges of the Taconics, Berkshires, and Greens in the distance.

Like the meadow below the main house, known as the Park, the sweeping descent of Crown Hill has been restored with great care. In Church's day the long hill was covered primarily with field cedars, white pine, maple, black cherry, and sumac, and growing around and through the trees were wild flowers and invasive shrub varieties. Church carefully curated this landscape, installing fences to restrict grazing, thinning out new growth as it arose, and periodically removing new saplings in favor of creating a parkland with various groupings of different tree species. Until the second decade of the twentieth century the meadow here was wildly overtaken by second-growth trees and invasive vegetation, and much of the view Church created was obscured until the first decade of the twentieth century, when the native meadow and sense of open space were restored.

Crown Hill Road was purely a pleasure drive, designed to induce a sense of awe and wonder for family and friends, offering a series of contrasting scenes in the landscape. It connects with Lake Road, and first loops around an old swamp before beginning a slow, winding, path up the hill and through the forest. At the top of the hill Church created a turnaround for donkey carts and carriages, and from the level patch of ground just before the terrain slopes dramatically downhill, is a bench that invites a good, long, meditation on the landscape at Olana.

According to tradition, Crown Hill was also known in the Church family as "Donkey Hill," the place where the revered donkeys were buried. No location for an animal graveyard has yet been established, but if you feel like tipping your hat in memory of these storied creatures, Crown Hill would be a perfect place to do so.

The *Plan of Olana,* 1886

In the summer of 1886, after having been suspended from the College of New Jersey (later Princeton University) for what a college official referred to as his "games and excitements," young Frederic Joseph Church turned his attention away from the apparently frivolous activities that had engaged him at Princeton and returned to Hudson. Having been enrolled in the School of Science and majoring in civil engineering, the twenty-year-old scholar now undertook a major project to create a comprehensive plan of his father's 250-acre estate at Olana.

Historian Ellen Lesser observes that while some of the mathematics in Fred's calculations were inaccurate, his *Plan of Olana* of 1886 "shows Olana basically as we know it today." That includes the house, farm complex, stable, studio building, vegetable garden, and carriage road system Frederic Church created that unifies the entire property. For Lesser, what is most important in Fred's plan is his detailed rendering of the tree plantings, both single trees and those in clumps, groves, and thickets. These show the hand of the famous artist now at work in the landscape, far from the canvas.

The importance of Fred's work will be evident to anyone who takes a tour of Olana, either in an electric vehicle or by foot, because the docents are never without an enlarged, foam core reproduction of young Church's elegant and highly detailed watercolor drawing. Though lacking experience and training, Fred succeeded in fully documenting his father's entire vision for the estate, and to this day the *Plan of Olana* remains instrumental in both the contemporary interpretation of the place and the restoration of the larger landscape. Although he was suspended by the college and never graduated, the young man

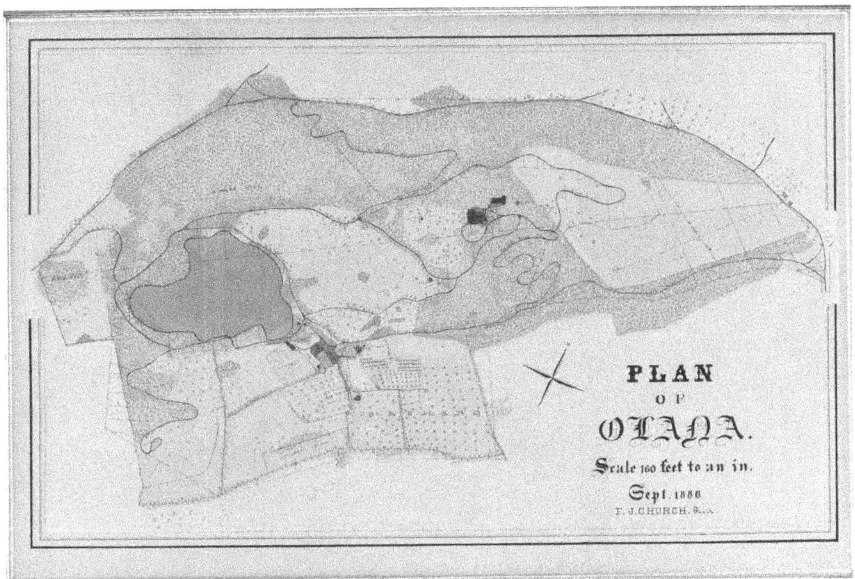

Frederic Joseph Church's *Plan of Olana*.

ended up producing what Lesser called "the single most important document relating to the landscape at Olana."

There is one mystery that still resides in Frederic Joseph's *Plan of Olana*: the designation of a "Summer House" on an open knoll just a few hundred feet from the main house. Also called an aedicule or "little house," this style of miniature architecture dates to the colonial period and by the nineteenth century had become a popular addition to American country estates. Alexander Jackson Downing was one of the prime boosters of the original concept of the "tiny house"; in 1852 he wrote that "the delight of gardens seems to be enjoyed more by looking at them from summer houses." These structures offered various perks in a landscape, not only as shelter from the elements and "agreeable resting places," as Downing put it, but as carefully sited viewing platforms. The intriguing label on the 1886 plan continues to engage the imaginations of researchers and artists; in 2016 The Olana Partnership invited twenty-one architects and landscape architects to envision a design for the elusive summer house and showcased their work in an exhibition and companion booklet titled *Follies, Function & Form: Imagining Olana's Summer House*. While no documentation about Church's Summer House has yet been found, you can

Mark Prezorski pauses an electric vehicle tour along Ridge Road, using the 1886 *Plan of Olana* to help interpret the landscape.

experience a few rustic examples in New York's Central Park: in the Ramble, the Cop Cot, or my personal favorite, the Dene, which is perched atop a steep rock outcrop of Manhattan schist, a relic of the last ice age, near the Zoo at Sixty-Eighth Street.

Standing at the top of Crown Hill, an elevation of 350 feet, is a fine spot to contemplate the story of young Church, his academic struggles, and his invaluable contribution to this place. From here you will see the house, farm, gardens, woodland, orchards, and the South Road as it snakes its way up the meadow—all elements that Frederic Joseph so meticulously inscribed in his *Plan of Olana.*

Buckthorn Fence

On an icy morning in January 2025, my brother Pier and I slip-slided down Crown Hill in search of a fragment of the fence Frederic Church strung across the middle of his meadow to restrict grazing in an area close to his new carriage road.

I knew from Robert Toole's authoritative and meticulously comprehensive *Historic Landscape Report* that Church had used a style of fence called Buckthorn, which was patented in July 1881 by one Thomas V. Allis of New York City. In a book about the history of fencing in America, Henry and Frances McCallum offer some insight into why Frederic Church chose buckthorn over the many other—and less expensive—types of barbed ribbon fencing that were available in the late nineteenth century: It was effective, it was strong, and perhaps most important of all, this New York City product was advertised as "handsome."

Using the map of Crown Hill from Frederic Joseph's 1886 *Plan of Olana*, which clearly shows the property's original fence lines and his own intuition as a farmer, Pier navigated by some sort of internal homing device directly to the spot in the field where a tangle of wire had been carefully rolled up and moved to one side, there to rust handsomely over the decades. Here we found long strips of the twisted, flat strip of galvanized steel known as buckthorn fence.

The story of fencing in America is actually quite fascinating, beginning as it does with a desire to keep animals and trespassers *out*. Over time, with the invention of wire fencing, settlers realized that barbed-wire fences were effective in keeping animals *in*. In their book *The Wire That Fenced the West*, the McCallums include a lengthy quotation from the vice president of the Worcester, Massachusetts, firm that pioneered barbed-wire fencing. He explains that the earlier, smooth wire fences may have been cheap and easy to erect, but they snapped in the cold, sagged in the heat, and "had no terrors for cattle": The cows simply "sawed their itching necks . . . on the smooth wire, in the acme of creature satisfaction, until the fence gave way." The buckthorn model was designed with a humane series of dull prongs, or lances, which could be plainly seen by an animal and wouldn't cut into the wool or skin. But, handsome and effective as it was, the buckthorn couldn't compete with the cheaper styles of ribbon fencing, and by 1900 it was off the market.

Thankfully there is a bit left at Olana. If you find yourself wandering around in

Buckthorn fencing in the Crown Hill meadow.

search of the buckthorn fence and a memory of Frederic Church's happy animals indulging their "creature satisfaction," you too can join the jolly club of "Barb-arians," the McCallums' word for people who collect old barbed-wire fences. Just remember: New York State law permits you to observe, but never to remove.

Landscape Furniture

Church's reverence for trees wasn't confined to the living, dead, and dying forms he found in the forest; he also imagined them as furniture that could provide visitors with a naturalistic perch for meditating on the views he had composed for them. Longtime ramblers in Central Park may recognize a familiar friend in these shapes; oftentimes when I am walking through Olana I think of Calvert Vaux, who with Frederick Law Olmsted designed New York City's great park, and who incorporated rustic architecture made from unmilled wood, primarily American cedar, in entrance gates, summerhouses, arbors, pergolas, fences, and even beehives and birdhouses. Vaux worked closely with Andrew Jackson Downing, who introduced rustic architecture to Americans in the mid-1800s.

Church also admired rustic furniture, and having painted the famous Charter Oak in Hartford, Connecticut in the 1840s, he later acquired enough twigs and branches to have a gnarly armchair made from this iconic tree. The sketch shown here, made in 1889, is Church's own design, and there is at least one photograph in the Olana archive of a family member, Louis Church, sitting on a tête-a-tête version of his father's bench, probably on Ridge Road in the 1890s.

Using Church's original design, The Olana Partnership engaged a local custom builder of outdoor furniture and woodland garden structures with the lovely name Romancing the Woods, to reproduce the rustic bench out of native mountain laurel (*Kalmia latifolia*), which is likely what he used for his designs; they have a hardwood seat and are placed throughout the property. There is also a reproduction of a rustic railing made of twisted stems near the carriage turnaround at the main house, which existed in Church's time.

One of the first of these contemporary rustic benches was strategically

Frederic E. Church sketch of a bench, 1889. Paper, graphite. New York State Office of Parks, Recreation & Historic Preservation. Olana State Historic Site. OL.1980.1579(V).

placed at the top of Crown Hill, offering a stunning view from on high of the Olana house in the distance and the meadow, park, and farm below.

Wildlife

An astute and patient observer will find so much life in these woods. In 1979 a study conducted as part of the application process for the building of a nuclear power plant in the Olana viewshed found 134 species from thirty-six different bird families in the region around Olana, including Inbocht Bay—Church's "Bend in the River"—and Duck Cove. Seventeen species of reptiles and amphibians were observed, as well as thirty-eight species of fish including goldfish, largemouth bass, chain pickerel, bluegill, American shad, alewives, blueback herring, striped bass, eels, white perch, brown trout, and redfin pickerel.

Frederic Joseph Church's 1886 *Plan of Olana* identifies the swamp area you pass by on the way to the top of Crown Hill; it teems with wildlife throughout the year, but especially in the early spring. If you're lucky, you might spot a hawk cartwheeling over the Park, the large meadow across from Crown Hill, as it searches the ground for a mouse or vole. If you come very early in the morning you might find a deer or a fox staring at you intently as you pass by, or a turkey hen leading her brood of poults, and while you won't necessarily see one, the steady drumbeat of a woodpecker is a frequent chorus in the Crown Hill forest.

The Park

The top of Crown Hill offers the best, most sweeping view of the meadow that slopes down Long Hill. This was one of the first parcels of land Church bought, and in the early 1860s he began planting trees: fruit trees, sugar maples, white birch, and native evergreens like pines, spruce, and hemlocks. The Park is the area where he used the nutrient-rich "muck" from his lake excavation project, giving his new trees "liberal doses of it" and delighting in how they thrived. Church continued to plant trees for the next thirty years, retaining a woodland

Two garter snakes, Farm Road, March 2020; deer, North Road, July 2019; Portia Munsun, *Sharp Shinned Hawk*, 2017, from the Olana exhibition "Memento Mori Mandalas"; family of geese, Olana Lake, April 2013; heron on the Olana lake, September 2024.

at the edges of the meadow so it was framed as a kind of ornamental feature in the overall landscape, but the Park also had a utilitarian purpose, since the field was hayed as part of the agricultural use of the Olana property.

In 1934 a severe storm, likely the hurricane that devastated New England, ripped through Olana and did considerable damage to trees, a consequence of the landscape's thin, long-ago glaciated soils. The storm left the Park more open, which Louis and Sally Church apparently preferred. They didn't replant the trees, and they even cleared some other nearby areas that Frederic Church had kept wooded, so the Park changed quite a lot after he died, which we see today in the contemporary landscape. In recent years the grounds crew from NYS Parks began mowing a path across and through the meadow, so visitors can take a slow walk down a hill filled with native plants and striking views. The "road" was not designed by Frederic Church, but it is entirely in the spirit of his artistic vision and is the only one at Olana that puts grass under one's feet instead of crushed stone.

Ellen Harvey, *Winter in the Summer House*, part of the 2025 outdoor exhibition *What's Missing?* Harvey's structure was an imaginative artwork designed to activate the site of a "summer house" that was depicted on Frederic Joseph Church's 1886 *Plan of Olana*, but for which no physical evidence remains.

Bethune Road (right) and Ridge Road (left) “abrupt in their windings” and “turning off . . . at sudden angles,” as prescribed by A. J. Downing.

SECTION 7: BETHUNE ROAD, 1864–1865

Bethune Road, sheer and heavily forested, winds its way down the west-facing side of the Olana ridge and ends at Route 9G. A visitor in 1872 recalled it as a "mountain road." This is the only walking path at Olana that does not permit vehicles of any sort, including the electric tour carriages, and it remains essentially as it was in Church's lifetime, except in those days it made a connection with the Oak Hill–Hudson Road (today's Route 9G), which led to the Catskill Ferry. A hauntingly beautiful path, it tends to be the least crowded part of Olana, a place of solitude and quiet amid a dense forest with striking elements of ice age geology embedded in the hillside.

Church's friend George Washington Bethune, a minister at the Dutch Reformed Church in Brooklyn Heights, purchased this parcel of land in 1861, and he confessed in a letter that he had doubts about whether a road could safely be cut into the steep west side of the hill. Bethune died two years later, so completing the road became Church's challenge—one that he apparently relished for its dramatic potential. The family used Bethune Road to make a connection with the Catskill Station, or Greendale Landing, where the ferry made its regular crossing.

New Yorkers may recognize the name Bethune from a street in the West Village, which was named after George Washington Bethune's mother, Joanna. She was an educator and philanthropist who dedicated her life to helping women, children, and the poor. Called a "trailblazer of organized women's benevolence," in 1806 Bethune cofounded, with Elizabeth Schuyler Hamilton, the Orphan Asylum Society, a shelter that provided education and a safe environment for children, and in later years she opened ten schools for children. Bethune donated a parcel of land on the Far West Side to the City of New York, which was used in the nineteenth century for a massive laboratory run by Western Electric and, later, Bell Labs. In the 1960s the sprawling complex was reconceived as affordable housing for artists and their families and become known as WestBeth, named after the two streets—West and Bethune—that it straddles.

Dead Trees

In the American forest we find trees in every stage of growth and decay—the slender sapling rises in the shadow of a lofty tree, and the giant in his prime stands by the hoary patriarch of the wood—on the ground lie prostrate decaying ranks that once moved their verdant heads in the sun and wind. . . . Green umbrageous masses; lofty and scathed trunks; contorted branches thrust athwart the sky; the mouldering dead below, shrouded in moss of every hue and texture, form richer combinations than can be found in the trimmed and planted wood. Trees are like men, differing widely in character; in sheltered spots, or under the influence of culture, they show few contrasting points; peculiarities are pruned and trained away until there is a general resemblance. But in exposed situations, wild and uncultivated, battling with the elements and with one another for the possession of a morsel of soil, or a favoring rock to which they may cling—they exhibit striking peculiarities, and sometimes original grandeur.

—THOMAS COLE, *ESSAY ON AMERICAN SCENERY*

Thomas Cole, *From Nature*, 1823, ink on paper. Courtesy Albany Institute of History & Art, gift of Edith Cole Silberstein, 1965.68.1.

A signature feature of the Olana forest walks is the presence of dead and dying trees, most of which the park's managers leave in the landscape. Thomas Cole had a reverence for dead trees, which he shared with his young student. They are a "striking feature in the scenery," he wrote, and are "exceedingly picturesque. Their pale mossy forms rise from the deep, stretching their contorted branches, and seem like genii to protect the sacred waters." But even more, he identified with trees on a human level. "They spring from some resemblance to the human form," he wrote. "Expose them to adversity and agitations, and one thousand original characters start forth, battling for existence or supremacy."

For folks who come often, these dying and dead trees, some still standing, while many are bent over or lying on the ground in varying states of decay, are like old friends: They change over the years, as we do, and show their age and mortality. They're a marker of time in the landscape, and they eventually topple over and provide valuable habitat to countless creatures, from small mammals and birds to insects, becoming a life force even after they have died. Two centuries later they also remind us, as they did the artists in the nineteenth century, of the sometimes devastating effects of the human hand in the wilderness. Cole was almost certainly aware that, after North and South lakes in the Catskills were dammed for industrial and agricultural purposes, the water levels rose and drowned the trees, creating the skeletal forms that he observed along the shoreline. One of his paintings, *Lake with Dead Trees*, from 1825, conveys the eerie, melancholy beauty he found in this scene.

During his career Frederic Church sketched and painted trees from all over the world: South America, Jamaica, Europe, New England, Canada, and the Middle East. He created small studies of chestnuts and hemlocks, lone specimens in the glow of moonlight, and majestic celebrities like the Charter Oak in Hartford, Connecticut, his hometown. Walking the carriage roads at Olana, it is impossible not to conjure in one's mind the trees he painted, especially the dead ones in *Rain Forest, Jamaica, West Indies* (1865); *Storm in the Mountains* (1847); *Christian on the Borders of "The Valley of the Shadow of Death" Pilgrim's Progress* (1847); *Moonrise (The Rising Moon)* (1865); and the iconic *Our Banner in the Sky* (1861), made in the early years of the Civil War, in which a dead tree becomes the staff of an American flag, whose stripes are rendered by the changing colors in the sky at sunrise. Historian John K. Howat calls this haunting oil sketch "a visual quotation of Francis Scott Key's *Star-Spangled Banner*."

Guerilla Art

I couldn't help but notice the odd and beautiful sculptural forms in the landscape of Bethune Road, and one day I met a man who comes here several times a week. He remarked on the peacefulness of the path, and on a beautiful October day with the sun dappling through the multicolored leaves, he asked me if I had observed the "artworks" in the woods. He then explained to me how they got here, the work of an artist who comes to this somewhat deserted part of Olana and makes his own sculptures from dead trees. In some works he uses large and small branches to create a jagged horizontal presentation, a kind of arboreal mashup, on a vertical trunk. In another he

Dead tree sculpture on Bethune Road, artist unknown.

has artfully placed one segment of a dead tree trunk atop another, so it becomes a sort of plinth for the exhibition of a fellow, now fallen, member of the forest.

One of the great joys of walking at Olana is encountering the art exhibits that can be found throughout the park each year. But this nameless guerilla artist works in an unsanctioned capacity, reminding us that artists are everywhere, always working in new and unexpected ways.

The Olana Eye SkyCam

In January 1900, Frederic Joseph Church wrote to his father from Hawaii, where he was manager of the Honolulu Photo Supply Company. "We have introduced here a panoramic camera," he wrote, "with revolving lense which takes nearly 180° in one picture, & we have had great success with it." It is not known which model his store was carrying; it could have been the No. 4 Kodak Panoram, which was introduced in 1899 and used a pivoting lens that produced a 142-degree image. Or it could have been the Al Vista, introduced by the Multiscope and Film Company of Burlington, Vermont, about 1896 and known as the "Rubber Neck Camera."

Frederic Edwin Church died three months after receiving his son's letter, but given his own interest in panoramic art, it's fair to assume that he was intrigued to learn that Frederic Joseph was engaged with this new technology. Of course we will never know, but I'm willing to bet Frederic Church would be enchanted by the "Olana Eye," a livestreaming camera fixed to a stanchion outside his studio in 2020. Oriented toward Inbocht Bay and the "Bend in the River," the camera tracks changes wrought on the landscape by weather, light, climate, temperature, position of the sun, river tides—all the forces that Church's hero, Alexander von Humboldt, so faithfully observed and quantified. Hour by hour, day by day, the "Olana Eye SkyCam" offers up a new type of immersive, panoramic experience that carries forward an artistic tradition Church himself helped pioneer. It is in operation at every hour of the day and night and every day of the year.

Frederic Church was a teenager when photography was invented, and even as he developed his skills as a painter using oils on canvas, the new art fascinated him. He collected thousands of photos, including stereographs, daguerreotypes, and albumen prints, and in his library was a seminal work introducing the new art: William Henry Thornthwaite's *A Guide to Photography,* first published in 1845. Thornthwaite's influential book, the eleventh edition of which Church owned, opens with a definition: "The art of making pictures by the agency of light may be designated under the general term Photography—a term derived, as is well known, from the two Greek words, *phos,* 'light,' and *graphs,* 'I write or delineate.'" In other words: *I tell a story with light.*

It was not until the twenty-first century that scholars came to fully understand the importance of Church's own collection of photography, which includes more than five thousand images that range from landscape photos of the American West to antiquities of the Middle East and rare pictures from South America, Jamaica, Europe, and Mexico. The earliest photo in the collection is a daguerreotype of Niagara Falls by Platt D. Babbitt, taken in the early 1850s, and

A dead tree near the lake at Olana.

Images from the Olana Eye Skycam, 2021–2023. Courtesy of The Olana Partnership.

the latest are from 1900. Thus Church's collection spanned the years in which the art of photography experienced major technological shifts, including, at the very end of his life, the new panoramic camera his son was so excited about.

The Soundscape

The soundscape around Olana, like the viewshed, has changed since the days the Church family was in residence here, but there are some constants. My personal favorite is the train horn, a sound that would have echoed through the landscape during all the years they lived here. The Hudson River Railroad was chartered in 1846; the first trains ran from New York City to Peekskill, and the entire line, from Manhattan to Albany, was completed in 1851, almost a decade before Frederic Church began purchasing the land at Olana. By 1873 there were sixty-eight daily trains, passenger and freight, running north and south along the east side of the Hudson River.

It is impossible to precisely describe what those old trains sounded like, but according to train buffs the tone of those whistles, which in the middle of the century were made by steam, were "haunting" and "mournful." Today it's a different story, because Amtrak trains that run on the old New York Central Line along the Hudson River have a common horn: the Nathan K5LA. Introduced in the 1970s, this klaxon was designed to play what has been described as "a cheery chord" consisting of a D#, F#, G#, B and another D#, one octave higher: a B major 6th. Or as my friend, jazz pianist Dan Tepfer, explained in an email, "if you want to be even more accurate, you could say it's a BMaj6 in first inversion." No matter what you call it, the train produces its own kind of music in the landscape. Bethune Road takes the stroller closest to the Hudson River and the railroad line, but the train horn is loud enough it can be heard from anywhere in the park.

If you were visiting Olana on a summer day when the windows were open and Isabel Church was playing the piano, you might have heard that same chord coming from her Chickering upright. One of the most fascinating documents The Olana Partnership shared with me is a spreadsheet listing all the family's surviving musical scores, many of which are marked with Isabel's name on the cover. It's a tantalizing document because it lets us imagine the music that once floated through these windows under her fingers: Beethoven, Chopin, Kalkbrenner, Mozart, Schubert, Felix Mendelssohn; arias by Bellini, Donizetti, Rossini, and Verdi; dances of every sort, from galops and gigues to quadrilles and waltzes. And then there is this treasure, a piece Isabel must have loved playing for her husband in the early years of their marriage: George William Warren's long, dramatic, endlessly upbeat *Marche di Bravura: Homage to Church's Picture "The Heart of the Andes,"* published in 1863, with an opening tempo marking of *Allegro energico* that proceeds through the moods of *Grandioso*, *Furioso*, *Vigoroso*, and, finally, *Elegante*.

Frederic Church was also a music maker and famously entertained friends during a large vacation party on Mount Desert in Maine that was organized by Charles Tracy in 1855. In his "Log Book" Tracy records how Church thrilled members of the party, playing a piano that had arrived on a sailboat—apparently "the first time such an instrument ever sounded" in this part of Maine—and singing songs. "Mr. Church's capacity for entertainment is perfectly inexhaustible," Tracy recalled. The great American piano virtuoso and composer Louis Moreau Gottschalk deeply admired Church and composed a *Mazurka poétique* in tribute to the man he called "the most gifted artist that I know, [and] the most sensitive to music." Gottschalk and Warren teamed up and created a four-hand version of the *Marche de Bravura* that was, according to the *New York Times*, "most heartily encored" when it debuted in the Brooklyn Academy on March 2, 1863.

Also included in Isabel's library, acquired in the last year of her life, is a collection of works by Cécile Chaminade, a prolific composer and pianist born in Paris in 1857. Like so many of the female Hudson River School painters of the nineteenth century, Chaminade's work—once extremely popular in America and abroad—became almost entirely forgotten in the twentieth century; only recently is it being rediscovered by musicians like Sarah Cahill in her three-volume collection *The Future is Female*.

The Churches had two Chickering pianos in the house, each with eighty-five keys: a square grand in Frederic's studio, purchased in 1849, and an upright in the dining room, purchased in 1885. Interestingly, while both pianos had fewer keys than a modern, eighty-eight-key piano, the older one had three fewer keys at the bass end, and the newer one had three fewer keys at the treble end. One thing we can be certain of about life at Olana: The house was filled with music.

Across the river, Thomas Cole also heard music in the landscape. The painter who made the Kaaterskill Falls famous felt that a waterfall "presents to the mind the beautiful, but apparently incongruous idea of fixedness and motion—a single existence in which we perceive unceasing change and everlasting duration. The waterfall may be called the voice of the landscape; for unlike the rocks and woods which utter sounds as the passive instruments, played on by the winds, the waterfall strikes its own chords, and rocks, and mountains re-echo its rich harmony."

The Olana soundscape today is rich with the call of birds, from small songbirds to soaring birds of prey. Walking in the woods has its own soundtrack, especially on a windy day when the tall pine trees whine and crackle as they bend. In the dead of winter, when the Hudson is filled with ice, the barges,

Frederic Edwin Church, cover for the original score of *Marche di Bravura* by George William Warren, 1863.

The 1885 Chickering piano in the Olana dining room.

tankers and Coast Guard ice cutters add a banging chorus as their massive steel hulls break up large chunks of ice in the shipping channel. Perhaps my favorite is the call of Canada geese as they migrate twice each year, going south in autumn and returning to the Hudson River Valley in spring. Like the Amtrak klaxon, their song is a rare sound that signals both coming and going, and it's a constant in the Olana soundscape.

The view from Frederic Church's studio window showing Rogers Island under today's Rip Van Winkle Bridge, the Hudson, and the Catskills.

SECTION 8: THE HUDSON RIVER SKYWALK AND ART TRAIL, 2019

When Frederic Church and Thomas Cole wanted to visit each other at Olana or Cedar Grove, they would ride down their respective sides of the Hudson River and catch the Greendale Ferry. Also known as the Catskill Ferry, this was a steam-powered boat that took thousands of tourists fresh off one of the Day Lines from New York City to the popular mountain resorts in the Catskills.

The-five thousand-foot, cantilever Rip Van Winkle Bridge opened on July 2,1935 and, according to recollections of the household staff, brought unwanted traffic to the area and "a severe intrusion into the views from Olana." But on a beautiful June day eighty-five years later there was much rejoicing as a "Parade of Paintings" formed on both sides of the Hudson River and met in the middle, just above the shipping channel. They were there to celebrate the opening of a three-mile pedestrian walkway that connects the homes and studios of the father of the Hudson River School and his famous student, continuing an artistic conversation that began in the early 1840s. Today you can literally walk across the river from one artist's home to another.

Leave yourself plenty of time, because the views from the bridge are enthralling no matter the season or time of day. During a recent bridge renovation viewing platforms were installed to enable long, meditative study of the landscapes that inspired the Hudson River School painters. Rail fans will delight at the frequent Amtrak and CSX freight trains that toot their air horns as they pass underneath the bridge, and bird watchers will be rewarded with a parade of bald eagles, red-tailed hawks, turkey vultures, Canada geese, American crows, and many other species.

In 2021 the Cole Site and Olana teamed up to present *Cross Pollination: Heade, Cole, Church, and Our Contemporary Moment*, an exhibition held at both historic sites that explored how ideas germinate among artists and how scientific observation and understanding, in the nineteenth centu-

The “Parade of Paintings” that opened the Skywalk, with Mark Prezorski (holding umbrella) and Sean Sawyer (at far right with cap) leading the way from Olana.

ry and the twenty-first, informed their work. The show also introduced modern museumgoers to the art of two long-overlooked artists: the exquisite ceramic work of Emily Cole, daughter of Thomas, and the exacting, beautiful botanical art of her friend Isabel Charlotte “Downie” Church, daughter of Frederic.

As one journalist described it, the show was “a potent contribution to the relatively new notion that artists like Cole, Church and Heade were proto-environmentalists whose art brought them close to the natural world they loved and, as a consequence, made them frontline witnesses to its devastation.” Contemporary works examining the loss of birds in North America were displayed alongside Martin Johnson Heade’s stunning paintings of hummingbirds. Other artistic juxtapositions highlighted issues around climate change, land stewardship, and the fragility of natural ecosystems. The provocative show served as a kind of cultural bridge between the two homes and highlighted the efforts of both Olana and the Cole Site to use their historic houses and landscapes as platforms for engaging art lovers with many of the key issues of the day—both in our contemporary moment and in history.

The Rip Van Winkle Bridge

When the State of New York announced plans to build the Rip Van Winkle Bridge in 1933, the headline in the *Knickerbocker Press* trumpeted how it would join the estates of two important artists in a "Romantic Link." The reporter reiterated this idea in the second paragraph of his article: "Romance will attend the building of the $2,000,000 Rip Van Winkle Bridge," which "will form a remarkable mile-long connection between the homes of two of America's foremost painters."

The name of the bridge pays tribute to another influential and much-loved nineteenth-century artist: the writer Washington Irving, author of the classic short story about a lazy Dutch American man, Rip Van Winkle, who goes out squirrel hunting in the Catskill mountains to escape his nagging wife, Dame Van Winkle. Rip ends up joining a rowdy group of men who are engaged in a game of ninepin bowling, and he drinks and carouses with them until he falls into a deep, long sleep. When he awakes twenty years later, the American Revolution has happened, and the world is vastly changed. Sadder still, Rip's loyal dog, Wolf—"who was as much henpecked as his master"—has disappeared. The legend of Rip Van Winkle continues to thrive in the Catskills, where annual events and festivals celebrate it. Hikers on Hunter Mountain will find what is billed as a "larger-than-life" stone tribute to Rip by Kevin Van Hentenryck, which the sculptor carved out of local bluestone that is some 380 million years old.

While best known for the artists of the Hudson River School, it was writers like Irving and James Fenimore Cooper who helped define the Hudson River Valley as a truly iconic region. In *The Pioneers*, one of Cooper's Leatherstocking novels published in 1823, the protagonist Natty Bumppo recalls "a place in them hills that I used to climb to when I wanted to see the carryings on of the world." Scholars have identified the spot as Pine Orchard, the future site of the Catskill Mountain House, just across the river from Olana. When asked what he could see from the rock ledge, Natty sweeps one hand around in a circle and replies: "Creation . . . all creation." Frederic Church, some forty years later, echoed Natty's sentiment in a letter to a friend, writing of Olana: "Almost an hour this side of Albany is the Center of the World—I own it."

An aerial view, looking southeast, of the Rip Van Winkle Bridge passing over Rogers Island. Courtesy NYS Bridge Authority.

Thomas Cole Site

THINE UNPITYING AXE

And is the glory of the forest dead.
Struck down?—Its beauteous foliage spread
On the base earth?—O! ruthless was the deed
Destroying man! What demon urg'd the speed
Of thine unpitying axe? Didst thou not know
My heart was wounded by each savage blow?
Could not the lovliness that did begird
These boughs dis-arm thine hand and save the bird
Its ancient home, and me a lasting joy! -
Vain is my plaint! All that I love must die;
But death sometimes leaves hope—friends may yet meet,
And life be fed on expectation sweet—
But here no hope survives—never again shall o'er me spread
Never again, the gentle shade of my beloved tree—

THOMAS COLE, CATSKILL, JUNE 22, 1834

I first came to know Thomas Cole through his writing, not his artwork. Of all the poets and writers who conjured their love of nature in the early years of the Industrial Revolution, when the hand of humankind was beginning to forever alter it, Cole is perhaps the most unsung. In both his poems and essays he wrote from the heart, expressing a true oneness with the natural world. A deep part of Cole's humanity was connected to Nature; in almost all of his work he expressed his reverence for it, as well as his acute sadness and horror at "this human hurricane" that would desecrate it. Art, for Cole, was a "Symbol of our common humanity," and one historian described his work as "sermons in paint." Another, the great scholar John Wilmerding, wrote that "through his meditations on American nature, Cole was able to articulate for his generation the physical as well as the spiritual power of his country."

When you arrive at the Cole Site in Catskill, the first thing you see is a sign headlined "Land Acknowledgement." "It is with gratitude and humility," the text begins, "that we acknowledge that at the Thomas Cole National Historic site we are learning, speaking, and gathering on the ancestral homelands of the Muhheaconneok, or Mohican, The People of the Waters That Are Never Still, who are the Indigenous peoples of this land." It is through exhibitions at the Cole Site that I came to know the work of many extraordinary Native American artists, including Kay WalkingStick (Cherokee), Brandon Lazore (Onondaga, Snipe Clan), Truman T. Lowe (Ho-Chunk), and Alan Michelson (Mohawk member of the Six Nations of the Grand River).

I also learned about the female branch of the Hudson River School at the Cole Site, women such as Susie Barstow, Julie Hart Beers, Fidelia Bridges, Sarah Cole, Charlotte Buell Coman, Eliza Pratt Greatorex, Mary Josephine Walters, and Laura Woodward, all of whom worked *en plein air* and explored landscapes around the world with as much energy, courage, and independence as the more famous men did. With its 2010 show *Remember the Ladies: Women of the Hudson River School*, the Cole Site became, as its director Elizabeth B. Jacks wrote, "the first known exhibition to focus solely on the women artists associated with the Hudson River School," and it was nothing short of a revelation to find the canvases of these long-forgotten artists.

For a music lover a visit to Cedar Grove is especially rewarding, for the house is filled with musical instruments: a guitar Thomas bought in Italy in 1842, a long flute that comes apart in three pieces, and a handsome, twenty-two-string wooden harp. Displayed near the guitar is the score for Mrs. Dorothea Jordon's "The Blue Bell of Scotland" ("Ah where and ah where is your Highland Laddie gone . . .), a favorite Scottish ballad Cole loved to sing to his family while accompanying himself on the guitar. Cole was not only a music lover, but he was also fascinated with color and its connection to music. In his journals Cole created charts in which he matched musical notes with color and colors with moods. My favorite Cole painting is the *Diagram of Contrasts*, a color wheel divided into twelve segments—the same number of distinct pitches within an octave in the Western chromatic musical scale—that he created in 1834. In his diary entry on November 5 that year Cole described what he called "the music of colours," and his belief "that colours are capable of affecting the mind, by combination, degree, and arrangement, like sound." He experimented with building an instrument that could *play color*, using keys that, when struck, would lift screens to reveal colored compartments.

The Cole House describes itself as "the place where American art was born," and along with presenting the work and life of Thomas Cole, who is universally considered the father of the Hudson River School, much of the work they do there is devoted to making legible the work of other important artists, including those who have been overlooked for centuries. All of this happens inside an artist's home, studio, and landscape. There is an energizing spirit in this historic site that puts old and new ideas in fascinating, creative, often beautiful juxtapositions.

When you go, leave plenty of time to wander in the beautiful new Cole Center, which has a particularly outstanding and diverse bookstore, along with coffee, gift items, handsomely produced editions of Cole's writings, and a display of his paintings.

Emily Cole

A great friend and likely mentor to Downie Church, Emily Cole was also an exquisitely talented botanical artist. In the late nineteenth century this was a field of art that was open to women, even while it was considered unworthy of men—"just" a craft, not a distinguished art form. In 2024 the Cole Site issued the first known publication of Emily's work, and in her foreword Elizabeth Jacks echoed the sentiment of scholar Ella M. Foshay of the Whitney Museum that "it is well past time that we take back the flower for what it is: a potent vessel for conceptual ideas."

But the main text of the book is written by Amanda Malmstrom, and it's hard not to be moved by her admiration for Emily Cole. Writing in a footnote that she refers to the artist as "Emily" not to diminish her achievements but instead "to distinguish her accomplishments from those of her extensively researched father, who is widely referred to simply as 'Cole,'" Malmstrom describes the pioneering productions of an artist who produced hundreds, if not thousands, of works of painted porcelain during her career.

Emily Cole was a founding member of the New York Society of Ceramic Arts, established in 1892, and during her career Malmstrom tells us she painted a wide variety of plants, favoring those that bear flowers or fruits: "Irises, orchids, magnolias, peonies, tulips, and cherry blossoms fill large pages as centered bouquets. Daisies, pansies, lilacs, and ferns decorate smaller scraps of paper and the corners of pages." Like her father and Frederic Church, with whom the Cole Site believes she had a direct relationship, Emily brought scientific precision and an artistic sensibility to her work and marked her sketch-

Emily Cole's teapot, cups and saucers, cream pitcher, and sugar bowl. Photo Pete Mauney, Courtesy Thomas Cole Historic Site.

es and paintings with captions containing her observations about color and other important details. She was also preoccupied with the entire cycle of life in plants, and her works depict not only flowers in full, glorious, bloom but also those with broken stems and falling petals.

When I walked home across the river from the Cole Site after visiting the first public exhibition of Emily's work in 2019, I recalled the astonishment I felt in the New-York Historical Society when I first saw the permanent collection of John J. Audubon's paintings of birds. Like Emily Cole, Audubon imbued his work with a deep understanding of and reverence for another life form. That combination of exactitude and humanity is what animates Emily's gorgeous work.

"I let the details and the mark of her paintbrush speak," Malmstrom concludes. "Despite the undeniable skill with which Emily captured the vibrant life of flora on pearly-white porcelain, her legacy, as an artist deeply engaged with nature and modern botanical and porcelain painting techniques, was largely erased. Taking a feminist lens to Emily's work, I hope to shatter the idea that 'women's work and 'craft' are less worthy of study, admiration, and attention."

The Hudson River

The River Indians, who settled in the Hudson Valley long before an English captain employed by the Dutch West India Company came upon it by accident in 1609, had various names for the great river that would eventually be named for Henry Hudson. *Shattemuc,* sometimes spelled *Shattemue,* is one; *Ca-ho-ha-ta-te-a* ("the river") was another, use by the Iroquois. The Mohicans and Lenape called it *Muh-he-kun-ne-tuk,* variously translated as "where waters are never still" or "the river that flows both ways."

In one of the only known histories written by a Mohican, Captain Hendrick Aupaumut recounts the story of how the River Indians' forefathers journeyed from the western part of the United States before finally arriving in this valley. "The etymology of the word Muhheakunnuk," he wrote "is great waters or sea, which are constantly in motion, either flowing or ebbing." The ancestors had found "many great waters" during their travels, "but none of them flowing and ebbing like Muhheakunnuk. . . . Then they said to one another, this is like Muhheakunnuk our nativity."

That marvelous word pays tribute to the tidal power of this river, which comes under the influence of varying forces including the earth's rotation (the Coriolis force) and the phase of the moon. During a very cold winter it's easy to see how the river got its name, as huge chunks of ice drift upriver, then downriver, over the course of a single day. I have observed this countless times myself, and also the stranger phenomenon of ice floes that appear to drift simultaneously in both directions, heading one way on the west side of the river and another on the east, a process called eddying that is not, in fact, connected to the tides.

We call it a river, but as historian Margaret Schram helpfully points out, it is much than that: "In her 315-mile journey," Schram writes of the majestic waterway we know today as the Hudson River, "she is a mountain stream, a canal, a fjord, and an estuary."

Rogers Island

The 281 acres of Rogers Island, which extends underneath the Rip Van Winkle Bridge and sits at the foot of Mount Merino, contains a surprising number of threads in the American story. It appears on one of the first maps of New York State: the one made by Adriaen Van Der Donck in 1656 of New Netherland, which identifies the island with a label in Dutch, "t'Vaste Rack." This word conveys what every voyager on the Hudson River knew to be the commencement of a certain "rak," or sailing course. Later known as Vastrix, or Vastrack, this island soon became a common marker on land deeds in the seventeenth century.

It is not yet known what the Indigenous people called it before the Dutch arrived, but we do know it was almost certainly the site of the last battle between two longtime rival nations, the Mohicans and their western neighbors, the Mohawks, in the second half of the 1620s.

According to tradition, the fight between the two Indian nations began on the western shore of the river near Catskill. As the day wore on the Mohawks, exhausted from the battle, fled to the little island on the opposite shore, where they built campfires and placed blankets over piles of sticks and logs, disguising themselves as sleeping warriors. "Cautiously the Mohicans crept upon the scene," a colorful 1884 newspaper article recounts, "and seeing the recumbent forms, as they supposed, of their careless enemies, discharged their weapons . . . the struggle was sharp, short and decisive." The year of the fight is still unknown, but as historian Shirley W. Dunn reports, neither Indian nation had yet obtained guns from the Europeans by the late 1620s, so it is likely this final battle unfolded with bows and arrows. Today it's not uncommon to hear accounts from duck hunters of finding arrowheads on Rogers Island.

It was in the years following this battle that the Mohicans entered into agreements with the Dutch to sell their lands along the Hudson River. And here Rogers Island enters the story again: In 1649 the first land deed recorded in Columbia County, dated May 27, 1649, established as one of its boundaries the southern end of *tien Ponts Eylant*, or Ten Points Island, another of its later names. The deal was made by the Sachem known as Keesiewey, and the payment he received from Brant Arent Van Slichtenhorst "with others," as recorded in the deed, was "10 fathoms of cloth, 10 kettles, 10 axes, 10 adzes, 10 swords, 10 hands sewant (strung beads), 10 knives, 1 firelock gun."

Rogers Island, as it came to be known by the middle of the nineteenth century, also contributed to the industrial powerhouse that was Hudson, New York. On historic maps a label at the southern tip identifies the Washington Ice Company. Incorporated in 1855, this was a major ice harvesting enterprise; when it was acquired by the Knickerbocker Ice Company in 1869 it became the largest supplier of ice to New York City. There are no photographs of the Washington Ice Company's factory, but in 1868 Thomas Cole's son, Theodore, who was Frederic Church's farm manager, sent a letter to the painter addressed to the U.S. Consul in Beirut mentioning that "The Ice House on the Island is a tremendous affair and is anything but Picturesque."

As always, in a quest to explore the deepest layers of history in this landscape, it's helpful to consult Robert and Johanna Titus, the Catskill Geologists.

In an intriguing article about the reconstruction of Notre Dame Cathedral in Paris, the Tituses suggest a connection between the land Notre Dame occupies on the westernmost of two elongated islands in the Seine River and Rogers Island in the Hudson. Both of them, technically, are what geologists call a longitudinal sand bar. "In fact," they conclude, "both of these islands are sand bars . . . an unusually large accumulation of sediment deposited in the middle of a stream." The heavy forest on Rogers Island suggests that the island has been here a long time, although it is not known precisely how long.

Picturesque or not, both Thomas Cole and Frederic Church painted or sketched Rogers Island, and it is prominently in view from Olana. In 1950 the whole island was made a wildlife preserve to provide refuge for migrating waterfowl. The best view at Olana is from the picnic area on Ridge Road, but looking down from the Rip Van Winkle Bridge will give you a bird's-eye view of the varied habitat on the island, which supports a great variety of fish, wildlife, and plant species including, according to the Department of Environmental Conservation, several rare plants. The island contains one of the largest tidal swamp forests in the Hudson Estuary and prime examples of freshwater tidal marsh and intertidal mudflat communities.

Hudson River Boat Traffic

The first human-propelled craft on the Hudson River was likely a canoe. In the era before the Europeans arrived, Native peoples in this part of the Hudson Valley made canoes from birch bark and water-resistant cedar logs. First the core of the log was burned by fire, then it was hewn and shaped by hand. The largest canoes could carry twenty people. According to the Columbia County Historical Society, the Mohican nation may have extended as far north as Maine, as far south as Manhattan, east to Connecticut, and west to Schenectady. The Mohicans, or *Muh-hi-kun-nuk*, were the locals who first welcomed Henry Hudson and his crew aboard the *Half Moon* when they dropped anchor near present-day Germantown in September 1609. Here Hudson's first mate Robert Juet reported in his journal, they were met by a "very loving people."

In the 1860s, after becoming Frederic Church's farm manager, young Theodore Cole would row his small boat across the Hudson River for his commute from Cedar Grove to Olana.

Church loved to watch boat traffic on the river, observing in an 1877 letter that it was "always dotted with steamers and other crafts." Well, not *always*; during the winter the Hudson often froze solidly enough that no ships could pass through until the spring thaw. An 1872 newspaper article noted that the ice around Rogers Island that year was up to nine and a half inches thick. It was Franklin Delano Roosevelt who signed an executive order on December 21, 1936, in response to severe freezing conditions that prevented barges carrying heating oil from navigating East Coast waterways; the order authorized the Coast Guard to implement ice-breaking operations to keep the shipping channel open.

It was not an easy decision for Roosevelt, whose family had a long tradition of ice yachting on the frozen Hudson. Historian Winthrop Aldrich learned in an interview with Albany's mayor, Erastus Corning II, that Roosevelt at first refused to clear the river. "In the wintertime, ice-boating is what we do down here," he told Corning, and if the Coast Guard kept the river open it would signal the end of that longtime family tradition in Hyde Park, a sport he was determined to maintain for his sons and grandsons. "No," FDR insisted, "the federal government will not keep the shipping channel open during the wintertime." When I asked Aldrich why this story is almost entirely unknown—even to archivists at the FDR Library and Home, whom I contacted in 2024—he told me that when Corning shared the story with him in 1981 "he noted that he had never mentioned it to anyone before our conversation because FDR stated unequivocally that it was 'off the record.'"

Eventually FDR changed his mind, and today a visitor at Olana will see—and sometimes even hear—all kinds of ships, barges, tankers, and tugboats as they crush through large boulders of river ice in winter. In very cold winters ice yachters can still be found sailing on the Hudson River near Athens, Germantown, and in the Tivoli Bays, sometimes reaching speeds as high—and even higher than—seventy-five miles per hour. During warmer months, the river is crowded with many other vessels, including cruise ships, jet skis, kay-

A full-scale replica of Henry Hudson's ship *Half Moon*, just before it sailed by Olana on October 18, 2014.

aks, freighters, canoes, and cigarette boats pulling tubers and water-skiers. If you're lucky you might catch Pete Seeger's magnificent Hudson River sloop *Clearwater* sailing by.

Icebergs

One of the most dramatic views of Olana can be had from edge of the boat launch at the Ernest R. Lasher Memorial Park in Germantown, just a few miles south. It's stunning all year long, but especially, I think, during a frigid winter when the Hudson is filled with ice. The large chunks of ice scattered in the foreground of my photo are about all the Hudson River can manage, even

An ice yacht on the Hudson River, near Hyde Park, circa 1900. Courtesy New York State Archives, Education Dept., Division of Visual Instruction.

in the coldest winters. These were pushed to the shoreline by barges and oil tankers, and while they are not technically icebergs, they do remind a winter visitor of Frederic Church's deep love for the massive, sculptural forms he witnessed, and painted, in the frozen North Atlantic in the summer of 1859.

"No sane person can call an Iceberg a landscape," Church wrote to his fellow artist Erastus Dow Palmer in 1890, but "there is plenty of raw material outside my window—just now—to study." No doubt he was looking from his studio at Olana down the steep hill to the Hudson where large chunks of ice were likely strewn across the frozen river and piled up around the edges of Rogers Island.

My favorite book about Frederic Church is *After Icebergs with a Painter,* the colorful, riveting account of a five-week journey along the coast of Labrador and Newfoundland by Louis Legrand Noble, an Episcopal clergyman who was Thomas Cole's pastor and biographer. Before setting sail from Boston,

A barge makes its way south in the shipping channel, cleared of ice, in Inbocht Bay, January 2015.

Church made an extensive study of the physical and optical properties of ice so he would be ready for the magnificent icebergs that lay ahead.

Like his traveling companion, Noble engages deeply and joyously with nature, detailing the dangers and thrills of "our grand hunt" for icebergs in prose that often seems to have been inspired by Herman Melville, whose *Moby-Dick* had been published just seven years before the minister and painter embarked on their voyage. "Our game," Noble tells his reader in the opening pages of the book, "is thou roving Ishmael of the sea . . . the wandering alp of the waves; our wilderness, the ocean; our steed, the winged vessel; our arms, the pencil and the pen; our game-bags, the portfolio, painting-box, and note-book, all harmless instruments, you perceive, with mild report. It is seldom that they are heard at any distance, although, at intervals, the sound has gone out as far as the guns of the battle-field."

"Icebergs! Icebergs!" cried a sailor, and what follows is a riveting scene of the boatman oaring through "fearfully rough water" toward a "grand specimen of architecture in the sea" as Frederic Church rides the swells and sketches, pausing only occasionally "for passing flocks of fog."

Church's sketches and paintings of icebergs are among his most haunting

Olana as seen from the Germantown boat launch, January 2025.

and magical. He painted one at midnight, as the sun set in an orange glow. In another, *Ice Falling from a Lofty Berg*, he captures the moment when the massive structure implodes, shearing off large boulders of ice and raining down smaller ones into the wavy sea where, for the purpose of conveying the scale of the iceberg and its terrors, a small boat bobs in the tormented sea. Another large iceberg looms in the background.

Noble compares the icebergs they encounter with great works of architecture: "a cluster of Chinese buildings, then a Gothic cathedral, early style," then the Colosseum and the Parthenon. The berg they witness exploding in "the convulsions of an earthquake" he names Windsor Castle. As they tossed on the waves the two men conversed, Church educating Noble about the geology of the Alleghenies and Cordilleras and describing his thrilling travel adventures throughout South America. As a powerful storm wreaks havoc on the ship, hurling ocean spray across the deck "as a whirlwind sweeps the dust," the two men take cover below the booms to witness it, "as one might watch a battle round the corner of a wall," observing closely from the safest spot they could find. And then: "Wrapped in heavy overcoats, and wet and chilly, we came, not withstanding, to enjoy it vastly." *C,* as he refers to the painter throughout, "fairly overflowed with fun and humor."

That is a quality we cannot glean from the composed landscape at Olana, the paintings and sketches of Frederic Edwin Church, or the spectacle of his glorious house at the top of the hill: an elfin sense of humor that infuses letters, books, occasionally even an artwork. Once, to poke fun at Martin Johnson Heade, a painter famous for his stunning portrayals of orchids, Church made a doodle at the end of a letter to his friend, describing it as "a new variety" of orchid that he christened "Diabolica Headensis."

Church turned his sense of humor onto his landscape as well. It was a work-in-progress that was never truly finished, a piece of art he began in his thirties and continued working on until his death on April 7, 1900. When a newspaper reporter asked him if he was the architect of Olana, Church's reply was both accurate and witty. "Yes, I can say, as the good woman did about her mock turtle soup, I made it out of my own head."

ACKNOWLEDGMENTS

I've had a home in the Hudson Valley since 1985, long before the restoration of Frederic Church's carriage roads began in the early part of the twentieth century. In those days you would drive up to the house and walk around it, reveling in the views that Church himself fell in love with as a young student who tramped around with his teacher, Thomas Cole, in the 1840s. Maybe you'd take a house tour, particularly if you had a guest who had never been to Olana before, and then you would get in the car and drive away.

So my first note of gratitude goes to the magnificent staff at The Olana Partnership who undertook the long, careful, project to restore Church's vision: the five miles of carriage roads that he regarded, toward the end of his life, as his greatest work of art. Working with their partners at the New York State Office of Parks, Recreation, and Historic Preservation, these dedicated staffers studied the original plans for Olana, and with the help of art historians, landscape architects, neighbors, politicians, conservation groups, and supporters from around the world, worked for some twenty-five years to return the 250 acres of Olana to the condition that Church and his family knew and loved. Today a visit to Olana begins with a walk through the landscape, up and around the seven carriage roads that open up views the artist himself composed.

At The Olana Partnership, my gratitude begins with landscape curator Mark Prezorski, with whom I've traveled these roads for more than fifteen years. I couldn't have managed to write this book without the enthusiasm, wisdom, history, and insights he has shared with me throughout so many seasons, both on foot and in Olana's dashing, donkey-white electric vehicles. Sean Sawyer, president of The Olana Partnership, contributed a tremendous amount of his time and knowledge to my project and like the rest of his colleagues was immensely patient with my endless questions. I'm profoundly grateful to Maggie Dimock, Melanie Hasbrook, Clare Flemming, Carolyn Keogh, and Blakely Kralovec for their invaluable help with my research. There was never a question they couldn't answer or at least address with a document, article, photograph, diary entry, letter, map, or book. To those staffers at The Olana Partnership who read early versions of my text: I'm deeply grateful for your thoughtful, intelligent, meticulous feedback.

At the New York State Office of Parks, Recreation and Historic Preservation, I thank Linda Cooper, regional director for the Taconic Region, for her careful reading of parts of my manuscript and for sharing it with several of her colleagues, who offered valuable feedback. I also thank Kelli Smith for her help in securing permission to use historic photographs in the book. One of the reasons Olana is the magnificent place that it is owes to the care and hard work of the Parks staff, some of whom have offices in the historic house and others who work in every part of the landscape throughout the year.

Two early readers, Ida Brier and Benjamin Swett, helped make this a better book with their incisive comments and deep understanding of Olana and its place in the American story. I am deeply grateful to them both. I also thank Dorothy Heyl for sharing with me so many resources and insights into the work and life of David Huntington. For their time in interviews and answering follow-up questions on a wide range of subjects, I thank Winthrop Aldrich, Rick Benas, Carl Petrich, and Loretta Simon.

At the Thomas Cole Historic Site, I'm grateful to Amanda Malmstrom and Kate Menconeri for their help with various research questions. Lisa Fox Martin, the longtime chair of the Cole House Board, died in March 2025. I knew Lisa for many years and was lucky to run into her and her little dog Kallie on Olana's North Road earlier that year. Despite the bitter cold, Lisa stopped to share stories with me about Frederic Church and his mentor Thomas Cole. She was brimming with enthusiasm, wit, and knowledge, and with her passing the Hudson Valley has lost a vital, visionary cultural leader.

I'm grateful to Tambra Dillon at Hudson Hall for providing a wealth of research materials that I was privileged to examine in that beautiful, historic building, and for answering numerous follow-up questions. Like so many music lovers who live in this area, I am profoundly grateful to Tammy for her extraordinary, innovative work as Hudson Hall's executive director.

I will treasure the new friends I made during the course of writing and researching this book, including Carlee Drummer, president of Columbia-Greene Community College, and Margaret Davidson, a longtime trustee at The Olana Partnership.

This is my second book with Fordham University Press/Empire State Editions, and I'm deeply grateful to Fredric Nachbaur, my editor and the director of the press, for his enthusiasm and support during every stage of this book's creation. It has been a great pleasure to work again with his outstanding colleagues: Will Cerbone, Kem Crimmins, Mark Lerner, and Kate O'Brien-Nicholson. I thank copyeditor Gregory McNamee for his meticulous and intelligent work.

I'm profoundly grateful to Peter Aaron, one of the most talented photographers working today, for his generosity in granting permission to use the stunning aerial photo of Olana on the cover of this book, and to Mark Lerner for his elegant design. The "Rambler's Map of Olana" is the third map Marty Schnure has created for my books, and I'm especially grateful to her for her patience, meticulousness, and creativity.

Many other people offered help and support to me during the course of my research, writing, and photo research. I thank, in alphabetical order: Ken Barstow; Olive Cadet at the New York State Bridge Authority; Charles Canham at the Cary Institute of Ecosystem Studies; Nikki Childrose at Columbia-Greene Community College; Michael Clark at the New York State Department of Environmental Conservation; William D. Caughlin, corporate archivist at the AT&T Archives and History Center; Geralynn Demarest at Columbia-Greene Community College; Robert Gould; Robert Hammond; Louisa La Farge; Pier LaFarge; Maryanne Lee; Virginia Martin of the Hendrick Hudson Chapter of the NSDAR; Laura Morrill at the Albany Institute of History & Art; Ronald Patkus at Vassar College; Thomas Shannon, the Germantown Historian; Nancy J. Siegel; Dan Tepfer; Diana Thompson at the National Academy of Design; and Ginny Umiker.

I'm grateful to my literary agent, Melanie Jackson, for her wisdom and support, and to my exceedingly patient and creative web developer Antonella Iannarino.

Olana would not be Olana without dogs; they have been here since the Church family arrived in the mid-nineteenth century. One day while doing research at Olana I was beyond delighted to discover that Louis Church had installed a doggie door in the entry to his apartment on the ground floor of the house, so his pup could come and go at will. I thank Clare Flemming for directing my attention to a small design detail I otherwise would have missed. My dogs Duncan, Bucky, and Spooner happily tramped here and swam in the lake, and they helped Ann and me make many new friends along the way. For their always cheerful welcomes I offer a special pat on the head to Augie, Aubrey, Baku, Bernie, Bill, Cooper, Fern, Kallie, Nicky, Paco, Riley, Romeo, Dooz, Sparky, Thandi, Trevor, and Zen.

But most of all I thank my longtime walking companion, Ann Godoff, for sharing these woods and carriage roads with me for the past three decades. Olana will always be our place.

NOTES

All letters, diaries, transcripts, and original manuscript material relating to Frederic Edwin Church and the Church family in the Olana collection are officially the property of the New York State Office of Parks, Recreation and Historic Preservation/Olana State Historic Site (NYS OPRHP/OSHS). I have included the full names of both entities in the first relevant endnote, but in the interest of space have abbreviated the names in subsequent notes, as indicated below. The accession number (OL#), as requested by The Olana Partnership, appears when available.

The Olana Partnership very kindly made available to me a sizeable database of correspondence, diaries, and historic and contemporary newspaper reports, some of which was provided to them by various archives, collections, estates, and nonprofit associations. I have included the names of those sources where applicable and noted that they came to me courtesy of The Olana Partnership.

NOTES TO THE INTRODUCTION

Page 1: **at the center of the world**: This evocative phrase is the title of Russell Shorto's magnificent book *The Island at the Center of the World: The Epic Story of Dutch Manhattan and the Forgotten Colony That Shaped America* (New York: Vintage Books, 2005).

Page 3: **The art element**: quoted in William L. Coleman, "How Frederic Church & Frederic Olmsted Joined Forces to Create the Modern American Park," published by The Olana Partnership, quoting from a letter to Charles Loring Brace on November 24, 1871, https://olana.org/olmsted-church/.

Page 3: **We were anxious**: Frederick Law Olmsted to Charles Loring Brace, November 24, 1871, quoted in ibid.

Page 3: **thank Frederic Church for both its placement and the base of the sculpture**: On Church's role in the placement and design of Cleopatra's Needle in Central Park, see ibid., and Sara Johns Griffen, "Frederic Church and Other Hudson River School Painters as Catalysts for the Conservation Movement and Their Legacy Today," 9, https://www.slideshare.net/slideshow/illustrated-talk-on-frederic-church-and-the-conservation-movement-by-sara-j-griffen/10890296.

Page 3: **launched the campaign to save Niagara Falls**: Frederick Law Olmstead credited Church with sounding the alarm about development at Niagara Falls. He wrote in 1879, "My attention was first called to the rapidly approaching ruin of its characteristic scenery by Mr. F. E. Church, about ten years ago. Shortly afterwards, several gentlemen, frequenters of the Falls, met at my request to consider this danger." Ibid., 8.

Page 4: **rapidly approaching ruin**: John K. Howat, *Frederic Church* (New Haven, CT: Yale University Press, 2005), 172.

Page 4: **the restoration and salvation of Niagara Falls**: Ibid., 173.

Page 4: **he was also a founder of the Travellers**: Ibid., 75, 118. This was a small American society not affiliated with the Travellers Club of London.

Page 4: **I have made about 1¾ miles of road**: Frederic Church to Erastus Dow Palmer, Olana, October 18, 1884, transcript at Olana SHS Courtesy Albany Institute of History and Art, McKinney Library, Erastus Dow Palmer Papers.

Page 6: **a summary image of the American landscape**: Franklin Kelly, *Frederic Edwin Church* (Washington, DC: National Gallery of Art, 1989), 59. Kelly's citation is to "Fine Arts," *The Albion*, June 6, 1860.

Page 6: **the status of an artist**: Barbara Babcock Millhouse, *American Wilderness: The Story of the Hudson River School of Painting* (Hensonville, NY: Black Dome Press, 2007), 55.

Page 7: **deep meaning of the real creation**: Ibid., 86.

Page 7: **a new picture by Mr. Church is as considerable**: *The New York Leader*, March 21, 1863, quoted by Sean E. Sawyer in "A Healthy Kind of Discomfort," April 10, 2017, https://olana.org/a-healthy-kind-of-discomfort/.

Page 7: **Yankee of Yankees**: David Huntington, "Introduction," *Frederic Edwin Church: An Exhibition Organized by the National Collection of Fine Arts, Smithsonian Institution* (Washington, DC: National Collection of Fine Arts, 1966), 20.

Page 8: **intrusions**: On the few "intrusions" in the Olana landscape, see Charles A. Birnbaum, "Managing Change at Olana: Preliminary Recommendations for a National Historic Landmark Cultural Landscape," The Cultural Landscape Foundation, January 2011. 6. Birnbaum's citation is to Robert M. Toole, Historic Landscape Report, Olana State Historic Site, New York State Office of Parks, Recreation and Historic Preservation Taconic Park Region, December 1996, 2.

Page 8: **I regret exceedingly**: letter from E. P. Meany to Church dated January 31, 1888, NYS OPRHP Olana SHS OL.1998.1.446.1 and .2.

Page 9: **attempt to harmonize the opposing forces of nature and culture**: Beverly Astrachan, "The Olana Landscape Garden: Frederic Church's Contribution to Wilderness Preservation" (MA thesis, Columbia University, 1995), 28.

Page 9: **in laying out his landscape garden**: Ibid., 2–3.

Page 9: **in allowing nature to regain**: Ibid., 28.

Page 9: **the first modern environmentalist**: Bill McKibben, *The End of Nature* (New York: Anchor Books, 1999), 194.

Page 9: **Americans had a moral obligation to plant trees**: Griffen, "Frederic Church and Other Hudson River School Painters." In her talk Griffen cites the work of Bethany Astrachan and her master's thesis.

Page 9: **harmonies of nature** and **never broken with impunity**: George P. Marsh,

Man and Nature; or, Physical Geography as Modified by Human Action (London: Sampson Low, Son and Marston, 1864), 8, 90.

Page 9: **the ravages committed**: Ibid., 43.

Page 9: **self-preservation requires us to restore the equilibrium**: Ibid., 103.

Page 9: **great political and moral revolutions**: Ibid., 47.

Page 9: **I like wood for architectural purposes less and less**: Frederic Church to Erastus Dow Palmer, Olana, June 5, 1884, provided to OSHS courtesy Albany Institute of History and Art, McKinney Library, Erastus Dow Palmer Papers.

Page 10: **a reflection of Church's awareness of**: Ibid., 3.

Page 10: **profound appreciation of nature**: Eleanor Jones Harvey, "Church's Cosmos," Olana Partnership, https://www.olana.org/churchscosmos/.

Page 11: **We are having splendid Meteoric**: Frederic Church to Martin Johnson Heade, Hudson, October 24, 1870, provided to OSHS courtesy of Archives of American Art, Smithsonian Institution, Washington, DC.

Page 12: **a feeling of sadness**: F. N. Zabriskie, "'Old Colony' Papers: An Artist's Castle and Our Ride Thereto," *The Christian Intelligencer*, September 10, 1884.

NOTES TO SECTION ONE

Page 16: **bedded chert** and **the sea must have produced**: Robert Titus, "The Abyss," *Kaatskill Life: A Regional Journal* 17, no. 2, Summer 2002, 58.

Page 16: **beautiful wife**: Robert M. Toole, *Historic Landscape Report, Olana State Historic Site* (Albany: New York State Office of Parks, Recreation and Historic Preservation Taconic Park Region, 1996), 56.

Page 16: **some twenty thousand years ago**: Various time spans are given for the period of advance of the Laurentide Ice Sheet. On matters of ice age geology I am following the scholarship of Robert and Johanna Titus. The period of "about 21,000 years ago" is their best estimate for when the ice sheet had reached its all-time maximum. See Robert Titus and Johanna Titus, *The Hudson Valley in the Age Ice: A Geological History and Tour* (Delmar, NY: Black Dome Press Corp, 2012), 42.

Page 17: **a kaleidoscope of visual situations**: Ibid., 97.

Page 18: **So much of American culture**: David C. Huntington, *The Campaign to Save Olana: An Oral History*, ed. Dorothy Heyl (Hudson, NY: Olana State Historic Site, 2009), 34.

Page 19: **staggered**: Ibid., 6.

Page 19: **On Church's photography collection**, see William L. Coleman, "What Was Photography to Frederic Church?," and Corey Keller, "To Bring the World Home: Frederic Church and Photography," in *Terraforming: Olana's Historic Photography Collection Unearthed*, ed. Sean E. Sawyer (Hudson, NY: The Olana Partnership, 2023), 7–8, 11–15.

Page 19: **a Bedouin Arab's spear**: David C. Huntington, "Olana: The Center of the Center of the World," in *World Art: Themes of Unity and Diversity*, ed. Irving Lavin (University Park: Pennsylvania State University Press, 1989), 3:770n7. The citation is to the *Daily Evening Transcript*, Boston, December 3, 1869.

Page 19: **a Yankee gentleman's Noah's Ark**: David C. Huntington, *The Landscapes of Frederic Edwin Church: Vision of an American Era* (New York: George Braziller, 1966), xii.

Page 19: **I was wasting my time**: Huntington, *Campaign to Save Olana*, 9.

Page 20: **See Olana this weekend**: this telegram dated November 5, 1954, from E. P. Richardson, then the director of the Winterthur Museum, to Russell Lynes of *Harper's* magazine, was included by Dorothy Heyl in a webinar for The Olana Partnership, "David Huntington and the Saving of Olana," April 22, 2020, https://youtu.be/B9ivrbo5n3c?si=Z31zy6WP2p_iVP4R.

Page 20: **began desperately photographing it**: Huntington, *Campaign to Save Olana*, 10.

Page 20: **this vast, half-claimed continent**: Huntington, *The Landscapes of Frederic Edwin Church*, x.

Page 20: **a domestic cathedral of the Transcendentalist mystique of American destiny**: David C. Huntington, *Frederic Edwin Church* (Washington, DC: National Collection of Fine Arts, 1966), 19.

Page 20: **America was destined**: David Seamon, "American Landscape Artist Frederic Church's Olana: Creating Harmonious Place Through Landscape Design and Domestic Architecture," in *Presenting Sense of Place to the Public: Background Planning for an Introductory Multi-Media Exhibit for American Landscape Paper Frederic Church's Olana* (Washington, DC: National Endowment for the Arts, 1992), 34.

Page 21: **His artist's hand** and **He was an archetypal American**: Huntington, *Landscapes of Frederic Edwin Church*, 10.

Page 21: **might well have been quickly sold and eventually dismantled**: Toole, *Historic Landscape Report*, 125.

Page 22: **almost single-handedly resurrecting**: Comments from Dorothy Heyl were made during an interview with the author, January 10, 2025, in Hudson, New York.

Page 22: **miraculously preserved**: This is a slight variation on what The Olana Partnership called the preservation effort in the 1960s on its website, https://olana.org/the-olana-partnership/.

Page 22: **Olana is not a girl**: Typewritten text of speech delivered by David C. Huntington at ceremonial signing of legislation by Governor Nelson Rockefeller to acquire Olana, June 1966. New York State Office of Parks, Recreation and Historic Preservation, Olana State Historic Site, OL.2012.1.358.A-.B.

Page 23: **made the comment that if the men**: Mary V. Thompson, "Early History of the Mount Vernon Ladies' Association," *George Washington's Mount Vernon*, https://www.mountvernon.org/library/digitalhistory/digital-encyclopedia/article/early-history-of-the-mount-vernon-ladies-association.

Page 23: **It was also the first campaign**: See "1860: A New Era," *Timeline: Historic Preservation at Mount Vernon*, https://www.mountvernon.org/preservation/historic-preservation-at-mount-vernon.

Page 24: **Olana Preservation succeeded in purchasing the estate**: The fullest accounts of the story of the saving Olana has been told in Huntington, *The Campaign to Save Olana*, and Robert Toole's *Historic Landscape Report*.

Page 25: **entity dedicated to advocating for Olana**: For my account of the saving of Olana, I have relied on Huntington, *The Campaign to Save Olana*, and David Schuyler, "Saving Olana," *Hudson River Valley Review* 32, no. 2 (Spring 2016), 2–26. I am also grateful to Sean E. Sawyer for his insights and a helpful summary of details about the evolution of Olana Preservation, Inc., to Friends of Olana to The Olana Partnership, which he provided to me in an email dated March 7, 2025.

Page 26: **Parks staff go through each one**: Details about the work performed by New York State Parks staff were provided by Linda Cooper in an email of April 21, 2025, and in comments from her staff to an early draft of this book, for which I am grateful.

Page 28: **comprehensive master plan**: For more on the Olana Strategic Landscape Design Plan, see the website of Nelson Byrd Woltz Landscape Architects, https://www.nbwla.com/projects/park/olana-strategic-landscape-design-plan.

Page 29: **constructed as a mass timber project**: Pansy Schulman, "ARO's Mass-Timber Visitor Center at Olana Brings a 150-year-Old Artistic Vision Into the Present," *Architectural Record*, November 29, 2024, https://www.architecturalrecord.com/articles/17236-aros-center-for-art-and-landscape-at-olana-brings-a-150-year-old-artistic-vision-into-the-present.

Page 29: **Monterey pine**: The Olana Partnership, January 23, 2025, https://www.facebook.com/OlanaFredericChurch.

Page 29: **the glass is virtually transparent**: see "Bird-Friendly Glass Inspired by Spider Webs: Arnold Glas," AskNature.com, https://asknature.org/innovation/bird-friendly-glass-inspired-by-spider-webs/.

Page 30: **I heard some sweet songs** and **description of birds in Church's letter from Columbia**: Frederic Church to Mrs. Joseph Church, Barranquilla, April 28, 1853. From the Winterthur Library, Frederic E. Church, letters from South America, provided to OSHS.

Page 30: **the earliest productions by Church**: Gerald L. Carr, *Frederic Edwin Church: Catalogue Raisonné of Works of Art at Olana State Historic Site* (New York: Cambridge University Press, 1994), 1:22.

Page 30: **Indian meal dough**: Church wrote from Hudson to Mrs. John Gaul, Jr. on January 8, 1888: "We keep a supply of Indian meal dough, which they ["a little flock of snow birds"] are very fond of." NYSOPRHP, OSHS, OL.1998.1.10.1, .2.

Page 30: **Otis Elevator Company**: Annik LaFarge, *On the High Line: The Definitive Guide* (New York: Fordham University Press, 2024), 112–14.

Page 31: **floating palaces**: "The Hudson River Day Line: 1863–1971," Hudson River Maritime Museum, Kingston, NY, July 30, 2016, https://www.hrmm.org/history-blog/the-hudson-river-day-line-1863-1971.

Page 31: **The year 1824 marked a turning point**: statistics from *The Tourist* and details about the U.S. Supreme Court decision in *Gibson v. Ogden* (1824) are from David Schuyler, *Sanctified Landscape: Writers, Artists, and the Hudson River Valley, 1820–1909* (Ithaca, NY: Cornell University Press, 2012), 9.

Page 32: **wore out many pair of boots**: Howat, *Frederic Church*, 10.
Page 32: **the mountain house was seen**: Rachel Wilmer, *Journal of Her tour to the Falls of Niagara the 26th of June 1834*, quoted by Nancy Siegel, *Remember the Ladies: Women of the Hudson River School* (Catskill, NY: Thomas Cole National Historic Site, 2010), 9.
Page 33: **one of the prominent things now pointed out**: *Catskill Examiner*, August 31, 1872, quoted in Toole, *Historic Landscape Report*, 57.
Page 34: **a fortress and "treasure-storehouse"**: Gerald L. Carr, *Olana Landscapes: The World of Frederic E. Church* (New York: Rizzoli International, 1989), 2. For the reference in Strabo, see *The Geography of Strabo*, trans. H. C. Hamilton and W. Falconer (London: Henry G. John, 1856), 270.
Page 34: **Doubtless this was the meaning**: John Ashbery, *Selected Prose* (Ann Arbor: University of Michigan Press, 2005), 266.
Page 34: **who came up with the name Olana**: Karen Zukowski, "A New Jerusalem," in *Frederic Church's Olana on the Hudson: Art, Landscape, Architecture*, ed. Julia B. Rosenbaum and Karen Zukowski (New York: Rizzoli Electa, 2018), 133, 152.
Page 34: **demons and spirits**: Roderick Frazier Nash, *Wilderness and the American Mind* (New Haven, CT: Yale University Press, 2001), 8.
Page 34: **deeply problematic**: Scott Manning Stevens, "Native Prospects: Indigenous Peoples and the Landscape-Painting Tradition," in *Native Prospects: Indigeneity and Landscape* (Catskill, NY: Thomas Cole National Historic Site, 2024), 13–14.
Page 35: **important to me on a deep level**: Kay WalkingStick (Cherokee), interviewed in ibid., 59.
Page 35: **Whereas Cole presents his viewer**: Ibid., 14–15.
Page 35: **reify our relationships**: Ibid., 16.

NOTES TO SECTION TWO

Page 39: **a picturesque grove of hundred-year-old hemlocks**: David Seamon, *Presenting Sense of Place to the Public: Background Planning for an Introductory Multi-Media Exhibit for American Landscape Paper Frederic Church's Olana* (Washington, DC: National Endowment for the Arts, 1992), 44.
Page 40: **the expenditure of road-building**: F. N. Zabriskie, F. N. Zabriskie, "'Old Colony' Papers: An Artist's Castle and Our Ride Thereto," *The Christian Intelligencer*, September 10, 1884.
Page 40: **the hill is very precipitous here**: Ibid.
Page 40: **bruised bodies** and **other quotations**: this story of the sixty-nine-day passage by the donkeys is recounted by Church in a letter to William Henry Osborn, August 31, 1869, NYSOPRHP, OSHS, OL.2003.26A-B.
Page 40: **a donkey fever** and they are wonderful creatures: Frederic Church to Joseph B. Austin, Hudson, NY, September 16, 1869, NYSOPRHP, OSHS, OL.1985.64.
Page 41: **festive green coats and red harnesses**: Valerie Balint, "The Hidden Olana," *The Olana Crayon*, Winter 2011–2012, 10–11.

Page 42: **she got the nickname as an infant**: William Coleman, "Isabel 'Downie' Church, Class of 1889: An Ancient Artist and Her World," Olana Partnership, October 21, 2022, YouTube, https://youtu.be/VUfm2nS1RwY?si=asihBXJRxY6z8IRC.

Page 42: **rigorous scientific vision**: Ibid.

Page 43: **landscape-driven design approach**: Sean E. Sawyer, "Partners in Design: Frederic Church and Calvert Vaux at Olana," *Hudson River Valley Review* 39, no. 1 (Autumn 2022): 66.

Page 43: **Downing articulated his love for asymmetry**: Quotations from Andrew Jackson Downing, *A Treatise on the Theory and Practice of Landscape Gardening, Adapted to North America; With a View to the Improvement of Country Residences* (repr., New York: Orange Judd Company, 1875), 56, 271.

Page 43: **The great charm in the forms of natural landscape**: Calvert Vaux, *Villas and Cottages: A Series of Designs* (New York: Harper and Brothers, 1864), 51–52.

Page 44: **in that it could be viewed**: Elizabeth Barlow Rogers, "Foreword" to Robert M. Toole, *Landscape Gardens on the Hudson: A History* (Hensonville, NY: Black Dome Press, 2010), vi.

Page 44: **natural in appearance without pretensions**: Robert M. Toole, *Historic Landscape Report: Olana State Historic Site* (Albany: New York State Office of Parks, Recreation and Historic Preservation, 1996), 79.

Page 45: **they present a jolly appearance**: Frederic Church to William H. Osborn, Hudson, NY, July 22, 1871, provided to OSHS Courtesy of Princeton University Libraries, Osborn and Dodge Family Papers.

Page 45: **It's a giant bulldozer**: Robert Titus and Johanna Titus, *The Hudson River Schools of Art and Their Ice Age Origins* (Bovina, NY: Purple Mountain Press, 2024), 12.

Page 46: **Susie Barstow was an avid hiker**: Nancy Siegel, Kate Menconceri, and Amanda Malmstrom, *Women Reframe American Landscape: Susie Barstow & Her Circle, Contemporary Practices* (Catskill, NY: Thomas Cole National Historic Site, 2023), 17, 61.

Page 47: **hiked in long, heavy skirts**: On Susie M. Barstow's modifications to her skirts, see Nancy Siegel, in reply to a question during the online talk, "Susie Barstow and Her Circle: The Women of the Hudson River School," Town of Clinton Historical Society, via Zoom, March 7, 2024, https://youtu.be/Pe4IQgafoJo?si=2O3c7QNrMWr24w4C.

Page 47: **No wonder that gentlemen have been shy**: Mrs. W. G. Nowell, "A Mountain Suit for Women," *Appalachia,* vol. 3, no. 1, June 1887, 181–83, quoted in Nancy Siegel, *Susie M. Barstow: Redefining the Hudson River School* (London: Lund Humphries, 2003), 76.

Page 48: **wooded buffer**: Seamon, *Presenting Sense of Place*, 22, 43-44, 124, 166.

Page 48: **splendid woods**: Frederic Church to William Henry Osborn, Hudson, October 25, 1857, NYS OPRHP OSHS, OL.2003.7.A-C.

Page 48: **Leader College of Distinction**: AchievingtheDream.org, https://achievingthedream.org/2025-lc-lcod/ and https://achievingthedream.org/areas-of-expertise/equity/.

Page 49: **child care desert**: Deborah E. Lans, "A Visit to C-GCC's Day Care Center and Two New reports," *Columbia Paper*, April 3, 2025, 1.

Page 49: **horizon points**: Toole, *Historic Landscape Report*, 201, fig. 26.

Page 50: **words like "brilliant" and "luminous"**: Evelyn D. Trebilcock and Valerie Balint, *Glories of the Hudson: Frederic Edwin Church's Views from Olana* (Hudson, NY: Olana Partnership, 2009), 49.

Page 50: **directly from nature**: quotes from Alexander Von Humboldt's *Cosmos* quoted in John K. Howat, *Frederic Church* (New Haven, CT: Yale University Press, 2005), 45–46.

Page 50: **a transcript of the scenery**: Frederic Church to Bayard Taylor, #15, 10th Street, May 9, 1859, Olana SHS, Bayard Taylor Correspondence, Letters to Taylor, Box A-Cr. Letter #1, courtesy Cornell Regional Archives.

Page 51: **then move them about like pieces of a jigsaw puzzle**: Barbara Babcock Millhouse, *American Wilderness: The Story of the Hudson River School of Painting* (Hensonville, NY: Black Dome Press, 2007), 96.

NOTES TO SECTION THREE

Page 53: **red-veined**: Robert M. Toole, *Historic Landscape Report: Olana State Historic Site* (Albany: New York State Office of Parks, Recreation and Historic Preservation, 1996), 56,

Page 54: **I can make more and better landscapes**: Frederic Church to Erastus Dow Palmer, Olana, October 18, 1884, Transcript at Olana SHS Courtesy Albany Institute of History and Art, McKinney Library, Erastus Dow Palmer Papers.

Page 54: **geological wonder**: Columbia County Historical Society, "Artifacts of Industry," 2020, https://cchsny.org/wp-content/uploads/2023/04/artifacts-of-industry_CCHS.pdf.

Page 54: **The escarpment dates to the Devonian era**: On the geology of Becraft Mountain, see Stephen Marshak, "Structural Geology of Silurian and Devonian Strata in the Mid-Hudson Valley, New York: Fold-Thrust Belt Tectonics in Miniature," New York State Museum: Map and Chart Series No. 41, 1990, 9; and Robert Titus and Johanna Titus, "Becraft Mountain, from the Columbia County Catskills Stories in Stone," *Columbia County Independent*, February 18, 2005.

Page 55: **wigwam on the summit of Becraft Mountain**: "Legend of Spook Rock," David Hart, Greenport Historical Society, https://www.greenporthistoricalny.org/the-legend-of-spook-rock/.

Page 55: **Some number of these deals were unfairly done**: In his summary of Shirley W. Dunn's book for the Columbia County Historical Society, "The Indians of Columbia County," Jim Eyre offers as an example of this the sale of Rensselaerswyck properties. Columbia County History & Heritage 1, no. 3 (Winter 2003): 7.

Page 55: **Recorded Land Transaction No. 57**: Shirley W. Dunn, *The Mohicans and Their Land, 1609–1730* (Bovina, NY: Purple Mountain Press, 1994), 292.

Page 55: **Becraft Mountain plant employed eight hundred men**: "Artifacts of Industry: Universal Atlas Cement Co. Factory Ruins," Columbia County Historical

Society, 2020 https://cchsny.org/wp-content/uploads/2023/04/artifacts-of-industry_CCHS.pdf.

Page 56: **tallest structure between New York City and Montreal**: Citizens for a Healthy Environment: A Project of the Native Forest Council, 2002, *St. Lawrence Cement: Understanding the Impact*, 9. The stacks of the proposed forty-story tower St. Lawrence Cement proposed would be 406 feet tall, and sited atop Becraft Mountain, they would have stood six hundred feet above the Hudson River. The Erastus Corning Tower in Albany's Empire State Plaza is589 feet high. For more, see William Drenttel, "Stop the Plant: The Failure of Rendering," *Design Observer*, February 23, 2005, https://inventionofdesire.com/feature/stop-the-plant-the-failure-of-rendering/3067.

Page 56: **"The Bullet We Dodged"**: Sam Pratt, "The Bullet We Dodged: How the Cement War Was Won," *Our Town*, Winter 2010 https://www.sampratt.com/files/ot-bullet.pdf.

Page 56: **Margaret Davidson reflected**: My interview with Margaret Davidson took place on March 20, 2025, in Germantown, New York.

Page 56: **The little mountain**: Mount Merino is 502 feet (153 m) in elevation.

Page 56: **a kind of Shepherd's Manual**: Robert R. Livington, *Essay on Sheep: Their Varieties—Account of the Merinoes of Spain, France, etc.; Together with Miscellaneous Remarks on Sheep and Woollen Manufactures* (New York: T. and J. Swords, 1809), 2.

Page 57: **Several farmers raised Merino sheep**: *History of Columbia County, New York* (Philadelphia: Everts & Ensign, 1878), 138–39, 367.

Page 57: **sculpted into a particularly comely form**: Robert Titus and Johanna Titus, *The Hudson River Schools of Art and Their Ice Age Origins* (Bovina, NY: Purple Mountain Press, 2024), 96.

Page 57: **rise in perpendicular forms**: John K. Howat, *Frederic Church* (New Haven, CT: Yale University Press, 2005), 49.

Page 58: **one of the most prominent features**: "Mount Merino, Greenport, Columbia County," ScenicHudson.com, September 17, 2008, https://www.scenichudson.org/success-stories/mount-merino-greenport-columbia-county/.

Page 58: **goods amounting to 500 guilders in beavers**: Dunn, *The Mohicans and Their Land*, 285.

Page 58: **they knew that their island home**: Tim Mulligan, *The Hudson River Valley: From Saratoga Springs to New York City* (New York: Random House, 1991), 49.

Page 59: **Entrepreneurs would be a better word**: Margaret Schram, *Hudson's Merchants and Whalers: The Rise and Fall of a River Port 1783–1850* (Hensonville, NY: Black Dome Press Corp., 2004), 20.

Page 59: **has remained intact**: Hudson Historic District, National Register of Historic Places, https://www.livingplaces.com/NY/Columbia_County/Hudson_City/Hudson_Historic_District.html.

Page 60: **only the right combination**: Schram, *Hudson's Merchants and Whalers*, 5.

Page 61: **one of the richest dictionaries**: City of Hudson, Columbia County, Historic Preservation, February 2007, https://web.archive.org/web/20090611151658/http://cityofhudson.org/content/Generic/View/34.

Page 61: **a fine example of Federal-style architecture**: See the "Statement of Significance" in the City of Hudson Multiple Resource Area, National Register of Historic Places Inventory Nomination Form, 11, https://npgallery.nps.gov/NRHP/GetAsset/NRHP/64000560, and the Jenkins House website: https://hudson-dar.org/history-of-the-robert-jenkins-house/.

Page 61: **clock face on the steeple**: Carole Osterink, "Time Stands Still," Gossips of Rivertown, August 5, 2018, https://gossipsofrivertown.blogspot.com/2018/08/time-stands-still.html.

Page 61: **Fitzgerald managed to escape**: For the story of Ella Fitzgerald's time in Hudson at the New York State Training School for Girls, see Russ Immarigeon, "The 'Ungovernable' Ella Fitzgerald," Prison Public Memory Project, October 29, 2014, https://www.prisonpublicmemory.org/blog/2014/the-ungovernable-ella-fitzgerald.

Page 62: **the largest land-based commercial-scale steelhead farm in North America**: Anne Pyburn Craig, "Trout Is the New Salmon: Hudson-Based Fishery Champions Sustainable New York Steelhead," *Chronogram*, January 22, 2020.

Page 62: **Curiosity Shop**: Details are listed in *The Volunteer, Published by the Ladies of Hudson, N.Y.*, April 12, 1864. A copy of this broadsheet is in the archive at Hudson Hall was made available to me during a research visit in January 2025.

Page 62: **Charter Oak**: Scott Manning Stevens adds another valuable perspective to the story of this celebrated American icon: "According to one source, a Native leader asked the settler owning the land on which it stood not to fell the tree, saying: 'It has been the guide of our ancestors for centuries as to the time of planting our corn; when the leaves are the size of a mouse's ears, then is the time to put the seed into the ground.' The Indigenous narrative, which first preserved the tree, is wholly absent in Church's depiction of it as a patriotic icon." *Native Prospects: Indigeneity and Landscape* (Catskill, NY: Thomas Cole National Historic Site, 2024), 24.

Page 63: **a baroque opera destination**: Joshua Barone, "A 'Rodelinda' Brings Promise to Handel on the Hudson," *New York Times*, October 22, 2023.

Page 64: **opera with the spirit of a band**: Joshua Barone, "In Upstate New York, Where Even the Opera Is Locavore," *New York Times*, April 18, 2025.

Page 64: **at least twenty-three studies**: Howat, *Frederic Church*, 69.

Page 64: **is intoxicated with Niagara**: Amelia Sturges, July 17, 1856, letter to her mother. John K. Howat's note reads: "Portfolio of typewritten manuscript, 169, Rousseau-Sturges Family Papers, Archives of the Pierpont Morgan Library." Ibid.

Page 65: **hacked away obstructive foliage**: Barbara Babcock Millhouse, *American Wilderness: The Story of the Hudson River School of Painting* (Hensonville, NY: Black Dome Press, 2007), 98.

Page 65: **Ruskin's error**: Ibid., 99.

Page 65: **My attention was first called**: Beverly Astrachan, "The Olana Landscape Garden: Frederic Church's Contribution to Wilderness Preservation" (MA thesis, Columbia University, 1995), 30, citing Frederick Law Olmsted, "Notes by Mr. Olmsted" in Special Report of New York State Survey on the Preservation of the

Scenery of Niagara Falls and Fourth Annual Report on the Triangulation of the State for the Year 1879, ed. James T. Gardner (Albany, NY: C. Van Benthuysen and Sons, 1880), 27–30.

Page 65: **The cheap fares bring a great many queer people**: Frederic Church to A. C. Goodman, Cataract House, Niagara Falls, September 2, 1858, OL.1983.1456.A.

Page 66: **the restoration and salvation of Niagara Falls**: Howat, Frederick Church, 173.

Page 66: **ancient relics of the ice age**: Titus and Titus, *The Hudson River Schools of Art and Their Ice Age Origins*, 36, 49.

NOTES TO SECTION FOUR

Page 69: **Feudal Castle**: Frederic Church to Mr. J. F. Weir, Hudson, NY, June 8, 1871. Provided to OSHS courtesy of the Archive of American Art, Weir Family Papers, #77–78.

Page 69: **I have laid out a new approach to the House**: Frederic Church to Erastus Dow Palmer, Olana, June 20, 1886, provided to OSHS courtesy of the Albany Institute of History and Art, McKinney Library, Erastus Dow Palmer Papers.

Page 70: **Doors opened at seven forty-five**: Barbara Novak, *Nature and Culture: American Landscape Painting, 1825–1875* (New York: Oxford University Press, 2007), 18–19.

Page 70: **America's longest painting**: Kilburn Mill, "The Original: A Spectacle in Motion: The Grand Panorama of a Whaling Voyage 'Round the World," New Bedford Whaling Museum, 2018, https://www.whalingmuseum.org/exhibition/original-spectacle-in-motion. Note that if you add the antenna, the Empire State Building stands at 1,454 feet; without it, the building is 1,250 feet.

Page 71: **a mise en scène**: David Huntington, *The Landscapes of Frederic Edwin Church: Vision of an American Era* (New York: George Braziller, 1966), 5.

Page 71: **panoramic paintings were ideally suited**: David Seamon, *Presenting Sense of Place to the Public: Background Planning for an Introductory Multi-Media Exhibit for American Landscape Paper Frederic Church's Olana* (Washington, DC: National Endowment for the Arts, 1992), 37.

Page 71: **large-scale depictions**: Ibid.

Page 71: **keep the street clear**: Huntington, *The Landscapes of Frederic Edwin Church*, 5

Page 71: **a vast climatic range**: Thomas Fels, *Fire and Ice: Treasures from the Photographic Collection of Frederic Church at Olana* (Ithaca, NY: Cornell University Press, 2002), 19.

Page 73: **brain gasping and straining**: Barbara Babcock Millhouse, *American Wilderness: The Story of the Hudson River School of Painting* (Hensonville, NY: Black Dome Press, 2007), 107.

Page 73: **as Church called it**: Robert Toole, in his *Historic Landscape Report: Olana State Historic Site* (Albany: New York State Office of Parks, Recreation and Historic Preservation, 1996), cites the source as F. N. Zabriskie, who in 1884 published an article titled "'Old Colony' Papers: An Artist's Castle and Our Ride Thereto," in *The Christian Intelligencer*, September 10, 1884, which described "the

Boght, (or Bend)." Toole further notes that "the term 'bend in the river' was also used to inscribe various sketches that show this view" (442n).

Page 73: **Arabian Knights fantasy**: Novak, *Nature and Culture*, 22.

Page 73: **How I have walked**: Rev. Louis L. Noble, *The Life and Works of Thomas Cole*, 3rd ed. (New York: Sheldon, Blakeman and Company, 1856), 81–82.

Page 74: **such was the law**: Ibid.

Page 74: **the nattily dressed ghost**: Tom Ogden, "The Ascension of John LaFarge," in *Haunted Greenwich Village: Bohemian Banshees, Spooky Sites, and Gonzo Ghost Walks* (Essex, CT: Globe Pequot Press, 2012), 20–28. On *The Old Sign on Tenth Street*, see Annette Blaugrund, "Edward Lamson Henry," in *Next to Nature: Landscape Paintings from the National Academy of Design*, ed. Barbara Novak and Annette Blaugrund (New York: Harper & Row, 1980), 18–22.

Page 75: **he worked at the famous Tenth Street Studio**: Church was a tenant between 1858 and 1887. Annette Blaugrund, "The Tenth Street Studio Building: A Roster, 1857–1895," *American Art Journal* 14, no. 2 (Spring 1982): 64–71.

Page 75: **an experiment intended to provide studios for artists**: *The Crayon*, vol. 5, January 1858, quoted in Blaugrund, "The Tenth Street Studio Building," 64.

Page 75: **softly lighted**: Charles L. Fisher, An Archeological Discovery of Frederic Church's First Studio at Olana State Historic Site, Columbia County, New York (Peebles Island, Waterford, NY: New York State Office of Parks, Recreation and Historic Preservation, 1994), 1–2.

Page 75: **Archaeological explorations conducted in the 1990s**: Ibid., 8, 16.

Page 76: **did not consider a work finished**: Seamon, *Presenting Sense of Place to the Public*, 58n.

Page 77: **a lake like sheet of water**: letter from Frederic Edwin Church to Amelia Edwards, Hudson, NY, September 2, 1877, provided to Olana SHS courtesy Sommerville College Library, Oxford, United Kingdom.

Page 77: **I never forgot that moment**: All quotations from Loretta Simon and details about her life and work were provided to me by Simon in email dated June 13, 2013, that she titled "Response to Annik LaFarge's Questions Regarding Olana and the PASNY Cementon Nuclear Power Plant Proposal."

Page 78: **Four nonprofits joined the group**: Sources for the details about the environmental groups that came together in the cement plant fight are Sara Johns Griffen, "Frederic Church and Other Hudson River School Painters as Catalysts for the Conservation Movement and Their Legacy Today"; and Prepared Testimony of Harvey K. Flad, Alan Gussow, and David C. Huntington, NRC Public Document Room, letter submitted by Russell K. Stover in Case 60006 and NRC Docket 50-549, Power Authority of the State of New York, Greene County Generating Facility, March 2, 1979, https://www.nrc.gov/docs/ML1927/ML19276F674.pdf.

Page 78: **the Google of the time**: Carl Petrich in an interview with the author, January 31, 2013.

Page 79: **a functional approach to landscape aesthetics**: Rachel Kaplan and Stephen Kaplan outline their ideas in *With People in Mind: Design and Management of Everyday Nature* (Washington, DC: Island Press, 1998).

Page 79: **When I interviewed Wint Aldrich**: All quotes from Winthrop Aldrich are from an interview with the author on March 19, 2013.

Page 79: **the crowning touch**: Loretta Simon, "Response to Annik LaFarge's Questions."

Page 79: **building the power plant**: Carl H. Petrich, "Aesthetic Impact of a Proposed Power Plant on an Historic Wilderness Landscape," Forest Service, U.S. Department of Agriculture, 477 https://research.fs.usda.gov/treesearch/27617.

Page 80: **It was also the first**: David Schuyler, *Embattled River: The Hudson and Modern Environmentalism* (Ithaca, NY: Cornell University Press, 2018), 4, 118.

Page 80: **my professional opinion did not matter**: Rick Benas in an email to the author of February 26, 2013.

Page 81: **an ever-increasing flood of knowledge**: Andrea Wulf, *The Invention of Nature: Alexander von Humboldt's New World* (New York: Knopf, 2015), 237.

Page 81: one beautiful knot: Ibid., 237.

Page 81: **splendid Meteoric displays**: Frederic Church to Martin Johnson Heade, Hudson, October 24, 1870, provided to OSHS courtesy of the Archives of American Art.

Page 82: **is difficult to categorize**: "History: The House," The Olana Partnership website, https://olana.org/history/the-house/.

Page 82: **The ensemble is breathtaking**: John Ashbery, *Selected Prose* (Ann Arbor: University of Michigan Press, 2005), 264–65.

Page 83: **Nature first, second, and third**: Justin Martin, *Genius of Place: The Life of Frederic Law Olmsted* (New York: Hachette Books, 2011), 157.

Page 83: **contrived to make the whole collection**: Marianne North, *Recollections of a Happy Life: Being the Autobiography of Marianne North, Edited by her Sister, Mrs. John Addington Symonds* (New York: Macmillan and Co., 1894), 2:209.

Page 84: **Could my little Mother's great part**: Downie Church Black to Charles Dudley Warner, Sept. 23, 1899, ESCP, OL.1985.54.1.A.

Page 84: **transforming the hardscrabble hill**: Zukowski, "A New Jerusalem," *Frederic Church's Olana on the Hudson,* 133, 152, 140.

Page 84: **translating from the French**: Ibid., 147.

Page 84: **there are details that nobody would see**: Carl Petrich, interview with the author, January 13, 2013.

Page 85: **known as the Ombra** On the word Ombra, see: Sean E. Sawyer, "Partners in Design: The Making of Olana House," *Hudson River Valley Review* 39, no. 1 (Autumn 2022): 67.

Page 85: **They are always looking out the windows**: Seamon, *Presenting Sense of Place to the Public,* 33.

Page 86: **You notice that I write**: Frederic Church to Erastus Dow Palmer, Olana, April 19, 1891, provided to OSHS courtesy of the Albany Institute of History and Art, McKinney Library, Erastus Dow Palmer Papers.

Page 86: **"ceremoniously" peel back the bark**: Jean Shin's description of *Fallen* is on her website, https://www.jeanshin.com/fallen.

Page 87: **armor-like**: Meredith Mendelsohn, "A 140-Year-Old Hemlock Was Lost. Now It Has New Life as Art," *New York Times,* May 3, 2021.

Page 88: **a great variety of different plant types**: Plant names in the historic mingled garden were provided by Bob Riordan (gardener), Ellen McClelland Lesser (consultant), Linda McLean (Site Manager), and Alice Platt and Robert Toole (Committee) in "Olana's Flower Garden: A Restoration Report," Draft 11/28/2001, 1–2.

Page 88: **the *mingled* flower-garden**: Downing, *Treatise*, 1st ed., 366.

Page 89: your garden: Isabel Church to Isabel "Downie" Church, July 19, 1890, "Landscape Research Report, Olana State Historic Site, Hudson, NY," Taconic State Park Commission, New York State Office of Parks, Recreation and Historic Preservation, August 15, 1986, 5.

NOTES TO SECTION FIVE

Page 91: **varied material in the composition of natural scenery**: Gerald L. Carr, *Olana Landscapes: The World of Frederic E. Church* (New York: Rizzoli International, 1989), 125.

Page 91: **contributes greatly to the beauty of landscape**: Thomas Cole, *Essay on American Scenery* (Catskill, NY: Thomas Cole National Historic Site, 2018), 11.

Page 91: **Mr. C. & Miss Hale marked out the road**: Emma Carnes diary, July 3, 1884, NYS OPRHP OSHS OL.2000.285.

Page 92: **very pretty and attractive gifts**: Susan Hale, *Self-Instructive Lessons in Painting with Oil and Water-Colors on Silk, Satin, Velvet and Other Fabrics Including Lustra Painting and the Use of Other Mediums* (Boston: S. W. Tilton and Company, 1885), 21.

Page 92: **very stiff and lame, but lovely**: Robert M. Toole, *Historic Landscape Report: Olana State Historic Site* (Albany: New York State Office of Parks, Recreation and Historic Preservation, 1996), 62.

Page 92: **getting out muck**: Thomas Cole diary entry, February 28, 1860, cited in ibid., 37.

Page 92: **not less than 5,000,000 loads**: Ibid., 59.

Page 92: **My muck seems wonderfully adapted**: Frederic Church letter to JC, May 13, 1864, NYS OPRHP OSHS OL.1998.1.7.1.

Page 94: **until the icehouse was full**: On the annual ice harvest at Olana: Norman and Donald June interview by Evelyn Trebilcock, curator, June 12, 2001. A transcript was provided to the author by The Olana Partnership.

Page 94: **then the highest price ever paid**: Franklin Kelly, *Frederic Church* (Washington, DC: National Gallery of Art, 1989), 164.

Page 94: **the Gothic style**: Toole, *Historic Landscape Report*, 48, from "Hudson Revised," ca. summer 1867.

Page 95: **elaborate bird feeder**: Ibid., 107.

Page 95: **my gardener measures 5 feet**: Church in a letter to Erastus Dow Palmer, October 21, 1885, transcript at Olana SHS courtesy of the Albany Institute of History and Art, McKinney Library, Erastus Dow Palmer Papers.

Page 95: **make the building settle into the landscape**: Interview by the author with Sean Sawyer, January 23, 2025, at Olana.

Page 95: **Simplicity and predominant character**: Andrew Jackson Downing,

The Architecture of Country Houses (New York: D. Appleton & Company, 1851), 43.

Page 96: **the color of all buildings**: Ibid., 202

Page 96: miraculous preservation victory: The Olana Partnership, https://olana.org/the-olana-partnership/.

Page 98: **a practical Yankee**: David Seamon, *Presenting Sense of Place to the Public: Background Planning for an Introductory Multi-Media Exhibit for American Landscape Paper Frederic Church's Olana* (Washington, DC: National Endowment for the Arts, 1992), 119.

Page 99: **an expression of an ideal**: Toole, *Historic Landscape Report*, 2.

Page 99: **a serious botanizer**: John K. Howat, *Frederic Church* (New Haven, CT: Yale University Press, 2005), 51. Morning glories: Frederic Church to William Osborn, Mexico, February 11, 1885, transcript at Olana SHS Courtesy Princeton University Libraries; melon seeds from Persia: Frederic Church to Martin Johnson Heade, Hudson, September 22, 1885, transcript at Olana SHS Courtesy Archives of American Art; roadside flowers: Frederic Church to his father Joseph Church, Bogotá, June 9, 1853, Transcript at Olana SHS Courtesy Henry Francis du Pont Winterthur Museum.

Page 99: **the farm pays**: Toole, *Historic Landscape Report*, 50.

Page 99: **spoils the beauty**: Frederic Church to Erastus D. Palmer, Farm, May 3, 1871, transcript at Olana SHS courtesy of the Albany Institute of History and Art, McKinney Library, Erastus Dow Palmer Papers.

Page 99: **the amount of plowed land**: these figures come from Toole, *Historic Landscape Report*, 51.

Page 100: **Glorious Motor Car**: Susan Hale, quoted in ibid., 116.

Page 100: **mimics the format and palette**: Eleonor Jones Harvey, *The Voyage of the Icebergs: Frederic Church's Arctic* Masterpiece (New Haven, CT: Yale University Press, 2002), 63; the painting is reproduced on p. 64

Page 101: **hope that you will like it**: Frederic Church to Isaac Hayes, May 3, 1862, transcript at Olana SHS courtesy of the Library of Congress Manuscript Division.

Page 101: **one of the few works Church mentioned by name in his will**: Gerald L. Carr, *Frederic Edwin Church: Catalogue Raisonné of Works of Art at Olana State Historic Site* (New York: Cambridge University Press, 1994), 1:9.

Page 101: **Freddies dog arrived by express!**: Diary Belonging to Emma Carnes, 1882–1883, 81. NYSOPRHP, OSHS, OL.2000.284. 81

Page 101: **good for bow wowel complaints**: Frederic Church to Martin J. Heade, August 25, 1876, transcript at Olana SHS, courtesy of the Archives of American Art, Smithsonian Institution, Martin Johnson Heade papers, 1853–1904.

Page 101: **everywhere in the park**: See also olana.org/dogsofolana/.

NOTES TO SECTION SIX

Page 103: **Mr C is making another drive**: Emma Carnes diary entry, August 28, 1885, NYS OPRHP OSHS OL.2000.285. (Note: I added a comma after "drive" for clarity.)

Page 103: **In Church's day the long hill**: This list of trees is reported in Robert M.

Toole, *Historic Landscape Report: Olana State Historic Site* (Albany: New York State Office of Parks, Recreation and Historic Preservation, 1996), 104.

Page 104: **Donkey Hill**: This information was passed along to members of The Olana Partnership in interviews with Donald June, who grew up in Cosy Cottage during the years when Louis and Sally Church lived in the main house. I am grateful to Mark Prezorski and Maggie Dimock for sharing this story and the transcript of an interview with June conducted by Evelyn Trebilcock, curator, on June 12, 2001.

Page 104: **games and excitements**: William M. Sloane to Frederic Edwin Church, Stanworth, Princeton, May 18, 1886, NYS OPRHP OSHS OL.1998.1.362.1.

Page 104: **shows Olana basically as we know it today**: Ellen Lesser, *Landscape Research Report: Olana State Historic Site* (Waterford, NY: New York State Office of Parks, Recreation and Historic Preservation, 1986), 20.

Page 105: **the single most important document**: Ibid., 23.

Page 105: **this style of miniature architecture**: Therese O'Malley in "The American Summerhouse: 'Amusing, Instructive & Friendly,'" in *Follies, Function & Form: Imagining Olana's Summer House*, ed. Mark Prezorski and Jane Smith (Hudson, NY: The Olana Partnership, 2016), 9.

Page 105: **the delight of gardens**: Alexander Jackson Downing, "Domestic Notices: Kiosques or Summer Houses," *Horticulturist*, July 1852, 339, https://archive.org/details/horticulturistj007alba/page/339/mode/.

Page 105: **agreeable resting places**: Ibid.

Page 106: **an elevation of 350 feet**: Lesser, *Landscape Research Report*, 14.

Page 107: **why Frederic Church chose buckthorn**: Henry D. McCallum and Frances T. McCallum, *The Wire That Fenced America* (Norman: University of Oklahoma Press, 1965), 209.

Page 107: **had no terrors for cattle**: Ibid., 17.

Page 108: **Barb-arians**: Ibid., viii.

Page 109: **unmilled wood, primarily American cedar**: Francis R. Kowsky, *Country, Park & City: The Architecture of Calvert Vaux* (New York: Oxford University Press, 1998), 115.

Page 109: **Vaux was influenced by Andrew Jackson Downing**: Jessica Sain-Baird, "The Story Behind Central Park's Rustic Architecture," *Central Park Conservancy Magazine*, June 15, 2017, https://www.centralparknyc.org/articles/central-park-rustic-architecture.

Page 109: **mountain laurel**: Toole, *Historic Landscape Report*, 85.

Page 110: **so much life in these woods**: Bird and fish species in the Olana viewshed are listed in *Final Environmental Statement by the U.S. Nuclear Regulatory Commission for Greene County Nuclear Power Plant proposed by Power Authority of the State of New York, Docket no. 50–549* (Washington, DC: U.S. Department of Energy, 1979), 2–28, 2–36.

NOTES TO SECTION SEVEN

Page 115: **mountain road**: Robert M. Toole, *Historic Landscape Report: Olana State Historic Site* (Albany: New York State Office of Parks, Recreation and Historic

Preservation, 1996), 43, citing a diary entry from Henry Q. Mack of October 30, 1872.

Page 115: **trailblazer of organized women's benevolence**: Dorothy G. Becker, "Isabella Graham and Joanna Bethune: Trailblazers of Organized Women's Benevolence," *Social Service Review* 61, no. 2 (June 1987), https://www.journals.uchicago.edu/doi/10.1086/644443.

Page 115: **she opened ten schools for children**: Sarah Bean Apmann, "Bethune Street: Tribute to a Remarkable Woman," Off the Grid: Village Preservation Blog, January 20, 2021, https://www.villagepreservation.org/2021/01/20/bethune-street-tribute-to-a-remarkable-woman/.

Page 115: **Bethune donated a parcel of land**: Sam Moskowitz, "The Origins of Greenwich Village Historic Preservation Street Names: Part IV," Off the Grid: Village Preservation Blob, July 20, 2019, https://www.villagepreservation.org/2019/07/30/the-origins-of-greenwich-village-historic-district-street-names-part-iv/.

Page 116: **In the American forest**: Thomas Cole, *Essay on American Scenery* (Catskill, NY: Thomas Cole Historic Site, 2018), 16–17.

Page 116: **striking feature in the scenery**: Thomas Cole, *Thoughts & Occurrences: The Journal of Thomas Cole* (Catskill, NY: Thomas Cole Historic Site, 2022), 19.

Page 117: **In sheltered spots, trees have a tranquil air**: Rev. Louis L. Noble, *The Life and Works of Thomas Cole*, 3rd ed. (New York: Sheldon, Blakeman and Company, 1856), 65–66.

Page 117: **dammed for industrial and agricultural purposes**: On the damming of North and South Lakes in the Catskills and Cole's painting *Lake with Dead Trees,* see Robert Titus and Johanna Titus, *The Hudson River Schools of Art and Their Ice Age Origin* (Bovina, NY: Purple Mountain Press, 2024), 56.

Page 117: **a visual quotation of Francis Scott Key's "Star-Spangled Banner"**: John K. Howat, *Frederic Church* (New Haven, CT: Yale University Press, 2005), 107.

Page 119: **We have introduced here a panoramic camera**: Frederic Joseph Church to Frederic Church, Honolulu, January 12, 1900, NYS OPRHP / OSHS, OL.1998.1.607.1. On the early panoramic cameras, I am grateful for the expertise of Ken Fox, head of Library and Archives at the Richard and Ronay Menschel Library, George Eastman Museum in Rochester, New York, who provided information about these cameras, with input from the library's technology curator, in an email of January 22, 2025.

Page 119: **at every hour of the day and night**: See olana.org/olanaeye.

Page 119: **The art of making pictures**: W. H. Thornthwaite, *A Guide to Photography*, 17th ed. (London: Simpkin, Marshall, & Co., and Horne and Thornthwaite, 1860), 1.

Page 120: **the importance of Church's own collection of photography**: Details about Frederic Church's photography collection can be found in William L. Coleman, Corey Keller, and David Hartt, *Terraforming: Olana's Historic Photography Collection Unearthed* (Hudson, NY: Olana Partnership, 2023).

Page 122: **By 1873 there were sixty-eight trains**: Carlton Mabee, *Bridging the Hudson:*

The Poughkeepsie Railroad Bridge and its Connecting Rail Lines (Bovina, NY: Purple Mountain Press, 2001), 21.

Page 122: **the tone of those whistles**: Dmytro Voznyi, "Sounds of Steam Trains: A Nostalgic Journey," https://bosshorn.com/blogs/blog/sounds-of-steam-trains?srsltid=AfmBOoqL3d7-yp1woRaeLkEg9p4R4i5bkj8vBfQmxbxfL7GY7ZqUrBLN.

Page 122: **have a common horn**: See "Amtrak Early Horns," Railroad.net, https://railroad.net/amtrak-early-horns-t83156.html.

Page 123: **the first time such an instrument ever sounded**: Charles Tracy, *The Tracy Log Book 1855: A Month in Summer* (Bar Harbor, ME: Acadia Publishing Company, Mount Desert Historical Society, 1997), 56.

Page 123: **Mr. Church's capacity for entertainment**: Ibid., 62

Page 123: the most gifted artist that I know: Frederick S. Starr, *Bamboula!: The Life and Times of Louis Moreau Gottschalk* (New York: Oxford University Press, 1995), 216.

Page 123: **most heartily encored**: "Amusements," *New York Times*, March 30, 1863.

Page 123: **both pianos had fewer keys**: I am grateful to Edmund Michael Frederick, who, with his wife, Patricia Humphrey Frederick, founded and runs the Frederick Collection of Historic Pianos in Ashburnham, Massachusetts, for his insights into this curiosity. According to Frederick, in the mid-nineteenth century, as the seven-octave range became the norm, some pianos were made with A to a range, others with C to c. By the end of the century, the A to a range became standard, but it looked strange having two black keys together at the top (F# and G#), so they added A#, B and C.

Page 123: **presents to the mind the beautiful**: Cole, *Essay on American Scenery*, 13–14.

NOTES TO SECTION EIGHT

Page 127: **A severe intrusion into the views from Olana**: Robert M. Toole, *Historic Landscape Report: Olana State Historic Site* (Albany: New York State Office of Parks, Recreation and Historic Preservation, 1996), 121, citing an interview with Helen Howe, formerly a maid at Olana, conducted by Kathleen Gray, September 5, 1991.

Page 128: **a potent contribution to the relatively new notion**: James D. Balestrieri, "Building Bridges: An Inside Look at the New Exhibition—Heade, Cole, Church, and Our Contemporary Moment," *American Fine Art*, November/December 2021, 40.

Page 129: **Romantic Link**: Francis P. Kimball, "Rip Van Winkle Bridge to Join Two Noted Artists Estates Cole, Church Properties in Romantic Link," *The Knickerbocker Press*, Albany, New York, June 18, 1933. Transcript provided by Olana SHS.

Page 129: **who was as much henpecked as his master**: Washington Irving, *Rip Van Winkle* (Philadelphia: David McKay, 1921), 18.

Page 129: **stone tribute to Rip**: "Rip Van Winkle Monument," Great Northern

Catskills of Greene County, https://www.greatnortherncatskills.com/attractions/rip-van-winkle-monument.

Page 129: **Local bluestone in the Catskills**: Robert Titus, "Catskill Bluestone," *The Catskill Geologist*, October 26, 2023, https://thecatskillgeologist.com/2023/10/28/catskill-bluestone-oct-26-2023/.

Page 129: **a place in them hills**: James Fenimore Cooper, *The Pioneers* (New York: Barnes & Noble, 2006), 285.

Page 129: **scholars have identified the spot**: Robert Titus and Johanna Titus, *The Hudson River Schools of Art and Their Ice Age Origins* (Bovina, NY: Purple Mountain Press, 2024), 11.

Page 129: **Almost an hour this side of Albany**: Frederic Church in a letter to Erastus Dow Palmer, July 7, 1869, Transcript at Olana SHS Courtesy Albany Institute of History and Art, McKinney Library, Erastus Dow Palmer Papers.

Page 131: **Symbol of our common humanity**: Thomas Cole, *Lecture on Art* (Catskill, NY: Thomas Cole Historic Site, 2021), 5.

Page 131: **sermons in paint**: Franklin Kelly, quoted by Dennis Anderson in "Frederic Church and the National Landscape by Franklin Kelly," *New England Quarterly* 63, no. 1 (March 1990): 172.

Page 131: **through his meditations on American nature**: John Wilmerding, *American Views: Essays on American Art* (Princeton, NJ: Princeton University Press, 1991), 16.

Page 131: **the first known exhibition**: Elizabeth B. Jacks, "Director's Statement," in *Remember the Ladies: Women of the Hudson River School, Nancy Siegel and Jennifer Krieger* (Catskill, NY: Thomas Cole National Historic Site, 2023), 5.

Page 132: **In his diary entry**: Thomas Cole, *Thoughts & Occurrences: The Journal of Thomas Cole* (Catskill, NY: Thomas Cole Historic Site, 2022), 3–7.

Page 132: **the place where American art was born**: Elizabeth Jacks, "Director's Foreword," in Kate Menconeri et al., *Cross Pollination: Heade, Cole, Church, and Our Contemporary Moment* (Catskill, NY: Thomas Cole Historic Site, 2021), 4.

Page 132: **a great friend and likely mentor**: Amanda Malmstrom and Kate Menconeri, *The Art of Emily Cole* (Catskill, NY: Thomas Cole National Historic Site, 2024), 27.

Page 133: **it is well past time**: Elizabeth Jacks, "Director's Foreword," 4. Jacks's citation is to Ella M. Foshay, *Reflections of Nature: Flowers in American Art* (New York: Knopf, 1984).

Page 133: **to distinguish her accomplishments . . .** : Amanda Malmstrom, "Catskill China Painter: The Art of Emily Cole," in Malmstrom and Menconeri, *The Art of Emily Cole*, 11–12.

Page 133: **Irises, orchids, magnolias**: Ibid., 13.

Page 134: **I let the details and the mark**: Ibid., 28

Page 134: ***Shatemue***: Franklin Leonard Pope, *The Western Boundary of Massachusetts: A Study of Indian and Colonial History* (Pittsfield, MA: Privately printed, 1886), 7n3; Charles Merguerian and John E. Sanders, "Trips on the Rocks: Hudson Highlands and Bar Mountain, NY," Duke Geological Laboratory, October 22, 1988, https://dukelabs.com/Publications/PubsPdf/OTR02_HudsonHighlands_sm.pdf; and "The Legend of Roger's Island," Local Sketch, *Catskill Examiner*, July 19, 1884, https://sites.rootsweb.com/~nygreen2/rogers_island.htm#:~:text=The%20 Mohican%20turned%20at%20bay,the%20fight%20were%20found%20here.

Page 134: **Muhheakunnuk**: Captain Hendrick Aupaumut's history is quoted at length in Shirley W. Dunn, *The Mohicans and Their Land, 1609–1730* (Bovina, NY: Purple Mountain Press, 1994), 36–37.

Page 135: **In her 315-mile journey**: Margaret B. Schram, *Hudson's Merchants and Whalers: The Rise and Fall of a River Port 1783–1850* (Hensonville, NY: Black Dome Press, 2004), 7.

Page 135: **t'Vaste Rack**: Adriaen Van Der Donck's 1656 map of New Netherland can be found at the New York Public Library Digital Collections, Lionel Pincus and Princess Firyal Map Division, https://digitalcollections.nypl.org/items/e99dfb50-79bb-0133-0c3b-00505686d14e.

Page 135: **What every voyager on the Hudson knew**: E. M. Ruttenber, *Footprints of the Red Men: Indian Geographical Names in the Valley of Hudson's River, the Valley of the Mohawk, and on the Delaware—Their Location and the Probable Meaning of Some of Them* (New York: New York State Historical Association, 1906), 48.

Page 135: **it was almost certainly the site**: Shirley W. Dunn, in *The Mohicans and Their Land* offers four sources about this battle, three of which point to the likelihood of it being Rogers Island, and one that identifies it as Wanton Island, a bit to the south (265n15). Other sources include "The Legend of Roger's Island" by historian Benjamin Bellows Grant Stone, quoted in Arthur G. Adams, *The Hudson River Guidebook*, 2nd ed. (New York: Fordham University Press, 1996), 220.

Page 135: **second half of the 1620s**: One of the key sources, the "Local Sketch" from the *Catskill Examiner* of July 19, 1884, lists the date of the battle as 1628, and another, reported in Arthur Adams, *The Hudson River Guidebook* (220) quotes the report of Wallace Bruce in *Hudson by Daylight*, which lists the battle as having occurred in 1625. The actual date is still unknown. https://sites.rootsweb.com/~nygreen2/rogers_island.htm.

Page 136: **Cautiously the Mohicans crept upon the scene**: "The Legend of Roger's Island." This is almost certainly the essay that Benjamin Bellows Grant Stone's wife refers to in a letter dated July 14, when she noted: "Bell writing in our room the 'Legend of Rogers Island,'" cited in a July 14, 1884 diary entry by Mary DuBois Stone, transcript at Olana SHS Courtesy of Vedder Research Library, Greene County Historical Society.

Page 136: **The Indian nations did not have guns**: Dunn, *The Mohicans and Their Land*, 97.

Page 136: **first land deed recorded**: Ibid., 280.

Page 136: **Washington Ice Company**: The Washington Ice Company label can be seen on the 1873 D. G. Beers map of Greenport Township in the New York Public Library Digital Collections, Lionel Pincus and Princess Firyal Map Division, https://digitalcollections.nypl.org/items/510d47e3-6854-a3d9-e040-e00a18064a99.

Page 136: **the largest supplier of ice to New York City**: James Trager, *The New York Chronology: The Ultimate Compendium of Events, People, and Anecdotes from the Dutch to the Present* (New York: Harper Resource, 2003), 200.

Page 136: **The Ice House on the Island**: Theodore A. Cole to Frederic Church, May 24, 1868, NYS OPRHP OSHS OL.1998.1.157.1.

Page 137: **both of these islands are sand bars**: Robert Titus and Johanna Titus, "The Final Destruction of Notre Dame?", *The Mountain Eagle,* December 12, 2024, https://www.theschoharienews.com/2024/12/the-catskill-geologists-by-professors_12.html#google_vignette.

Page 137: **one of the largest tidal swamp forests**: Details about the wildlife and terrain of Rogers Island can be found on the DEC website: https://dec.ny.gov/places/rogers-island-wildlife-management-area.

Page 137: **water-resistant cedar logs**: Jim Eyre, "Where They Came From and What They Were," *Columbia County History & Heritage* 1, no. 3 (Winter 2003): 4.

Page 137: **very loving people**: Robert Juet, *Extract from the Journal of the Voyage of the Half-Moon, Henry Hudson, Master, From the Netherlands to the Coast of North-America in the Year1609*, Library of Congress, 326, http://hdl.loc.gov/loc.gdc/gckb.008.

Page 138: **Theodore Cole would row**: I am grateful to Michaela Ellison-Davidson for the opportunity to read her fascinating report, "Theodore A. Cole: Remembering a Legacy Through Art, Land, and Prose," written during her fellowship at the Thomas Cole Historic Site in 2023–24.

Page 138: **always dotted with steamers and other craft**: Frederic Edwin Church to Amelia Edwards, Hudson, September 2, 1877, transcript at Olana SHS courtesy of the Sommerville College Library, Oxford, United Kingdom.

Page 138: **ice around Rogers Island**: "The Ice Harvest on the Hudson," *Rockland County Messenger,* January 18, 1872.

Page 138: **signed an executive order**: Franklin D. Roosevelt's Executive Order 7521, authorizing the use of vessels for ice-breaking operations, can be found at the American Presidency Project, https://www.presidency.ucsb.edu/documents/executive-order-7521-use-vessels-for-ice-breaking-operations-channels-and-harbors.

Page 138: **In the wintertime, ice-boating is what we do** and **the federal government will not**: Nina Schutzman, "FDR Library and Museum Displaying Ice Yacht Expo," *Poughkeepsie Journal,* December 21, 2014.

Page 138: **When I asked Aldrich**: Email from Winthrop Aldrich to the author, December 30, 2024.

Page 138: **reaching speeds as high**: Reed Sparling, "Racing Faster Than a Speeding Car on the Frozen Hudson," https://www.scenichudson.org/viewfinder/iceboating/.

Page 140: **No sane person can call**: Frederic Church to Erastus Dow Palmer, Olana, December 28, 1890, transcript at Olana SHS Courtesy Albany Institute of History and Art, McKinney Library, Erastus Dow Palmer Papers.

Page 141: **Church made an extensive study**: Eleanor Jones Harvey, "Church's Cosmos," Olana.org, https://olana.org/churchscosmos/.

Page 141: **often seems to have been inspired by Herman Melville**: *Moby-Dick* was published in New York in November 1851; Church and Noble departed Halifax on June 17, 1859.

Page 141: **our grand hunt** and **other quotations**: Louis Legrand Noble, *After Icebergs with a Painter: A Summer Voyage to Labrador and Around Newfoundland* (Catskill, NY: Black Dome Press, 2022), 3, 20, 3.

Page 141: **Icebergs! Icebergs**: Quotations from ibid., 19, 38.

Page 143: **as a whirlwind sweeps the dust**: quotations from ibid., 59, 132, 144.

Page 143: **Diabolica Headensis**: Frederic Church to Martin Johnson Heade, December 22, 1881, transcript at Olana SHS, courtesy Archives of American Art, Smithsonian Institution, Martin Johnson Heade papers, 1853–1904. A photo of this letter appears on page 56 of the *Cross Pollination* catalog.

Page 143: **I made it out of my own head**: Toole, *Historic Landscape Report*, 54n266, citing Frank J. Bonnelle, *Sunday Herald*, Boston, September 7, 1890.

BIBLIOGRAPHY

Adams, Arthur G. *The Hudson River Guidebook.* 2nd ed. New York: Fordham University Press, 1996.

Ashbery, John. *Selected Prose.* Ann Arbor: University of Michigan Press, 2005.

Astrachan, Beverly. "The Olana Landscape Garden: Frederic Church's Contribution to Wilderness Preservation." MA thesis, Columbia University, 1995.

Birnbaum, Charles A. "Managing Change at Olana: Preliminary Recommendations for a National Historic Landmark Cultural Landscape." The Cultural Landscape Foundation, January 2011.

Blaugrund, Annette. "The Tenth Street Studio Building: A Roster." *American Art Journal* 14, no. 2 (Spring 1982): 64–71.

Carr, Gerald L. *Frederic Edwin Church: Catalogue Raisonné of Works of Art at Olana State Historic Site.* New York: Cambridge University Press, 1994.

———. *Olana Landscapes: The World of Frederic E. Church.* New York: Rizzoli International, 1989.

Cole, Thomas. *Essay on American Scenery.* Catskill, NY: Thomas Cole Historic Site, 2018.

———. *Lecture on Art.* Catskill, NY: Thomas Cole Historic Site, 2021.

———. *Thoughts & Occurrences: The Journal of Thomas Cole.* Catskill, NY: Thomas Cole Historic Site, 2022.

Coleman, William L. "How Frederic Church & Frederic Olmsted Joined Forces to Create the Modern American Park." https://olana.org/olmsted-church/.

Downing, Alexander Jackson. *A Treatise on the Theory and Practice of Landscape Gardening, Adapted to North America; With a View to the Improvement of Country Residences.* New York: Wiley and Putnam, 1841.

———. *A Treatise on the Theory and Practice of Landscape Gardening, Adapted to North America; With a View to the Improvement of Country Residences.* 2nd ed. New York: Wiley and Putnam, 1844.

Dunn, Shirley W. *The Mohicans and Their Land, 1609–1730.* Bovina, NY: Purple Mountain Press, 1994.

Fels, Thomas. *Fire and Ice: Treasures from the Photographic Collection of Frederic Church at Olana.* Ithaca, NY: Cornell University Press, 2002.

Griffen, Sara Johns. "Frederic Church and Other Hudson River School Painters as Catalysts for the Conservation Movement and Their Legacy Today." Talk at the University at Albany Foundation Albany Institute of History and Art, September 2009.

Harvey, Eleonor Jones. "Church's Cosmos." https://www.olana.org/churchscosmos/.

———. *The Voyage of the Icebergs: Frederic Church's Arctic Masterpiece.* New Haven, CT: Yale University Press, 2002.

Helmer, William F. *Rip Van Winkle Railroads.* Hensonville, NY: Black Dome Press, 1999.

Henshaw, Robert E., ed. *Environmental History of the Hudson River: Human Uses That Changed the Ecology, Ecology That Changed the Human Uses.* Albany: State University of New York Press, 2011.

Howat, John K. *Frederic Church.* New Haven, CT: Yale University Press, 2005.

Huntington, David C. *The Campaign to Save Olana: An Oral History.* Ed. Dorothy Heyl. Hudson, NY: Olana State Historic Site, 2009.

———. *Frederic Edwin Church.* Washington, DC: National Collection of Fine Arts, 1966.

———. *The Landscapes of Frederic Edwin Church: Vision of an American Era.* New York: George Braziller, 1966.

———. "Olana: The Center of the Center of the World." In *World Art: Themes of Unity and Diversity*, ed. Irving Lavin, 3:767–75. University Park: Pennsylvania State University Press, 1989.

Kaplan, Rachel, and Stephen Kaplan. *With People in Mind: Design and Management of Everyday Nature.* Washington, DC: Island Press, 1998.

Kelly, Franklin. *Frederic Church.* Washington, DC: National Gallery of Art, 1989.

Kowsky, Francis R. *Country, Park & City: The Architecture of Calvert Vaux.* New York: Oxford University Press, 1998.

LaFarge, Annik. *On the High Line: The Definitive Guide.* New York: Fordham University Press, 2024.

Lesser, Ellen. *Landscape Research Report: Olana State Historic Site.* Waterford, NY: New York State Office of Parks, Recreation and Historic Preservation, 1986.

Livingston, Robert R. *Essay on Sheep: Their Varieties—Account of the Merinoes of Spain, France, etc.; Together with Miscellaneous Remarks on Sheep and Woollen Manufactures.* New York: T. and J. Swords, 1809.

Mabee, Carlton. *Bridging the Hudson: The Poughkeepsie Railroad Bridge and Its Connecting Rail Lines.* Bovina, NY: Purple Mountain Press, 2001.

Malmstrom, Amanda, and Kate Menconeri. *The Art of Emily Cole.* Catskill, NY: Thomas Cole Historic Site, 2024.

Marsh, George P. *Man and Nature; or, Physical Geography as Modified by Human Action.* London: Sampson Low, Son and Marston, 1864.

Martin, Justin. *Genius of Place: The Life of Frederic Law Olmsted.* New York: Hachette Books, 2011.

McCallum, Henry D., and Frances T. McCallum. *The Wire That Fenced America.* Norman: University of Oklahoma Press, 1965.

Menconeri, Kate, Julia Rosenbaum, Mindy N. Besaw, and William L. Coleman. *Cross Pollination: Heade, Cole, Church, and Our Contemporary Moment.* Catskill, NY: Thomas Cole Historic Site, 2021.

Millhouse, Barbara Babcock. *American Wilderness: The Story of the Hudson River School of Painting.* Hensonville, NY: Black Dome Press, 2007.

Mulligan, Tim. *The Hudson River Valley: From Saratoga Springs to New York City.* New York: Random House, 1991.

Nash, Roderick Frazier. *Wilderness and the American Mind.* New Haven, CT: Yale University Press, 2001.

Noble, Louis Legrand. *After Icebergs with a Painter: A Summer Voyage to Labrador and Around Newfoundland*. Catskill, NY: Black Dome Press, 2022.

Novak, Barbara. *Nature and Culture: American Landscape and Painting, 1825–1875*. New York: Oxford University Press, 2007.

Novak, Barbara, and Annette Blaugrund, eds. *Next to Nature: Landscape Paintings from the National Academy of Design*. New York: Harper & Row, 1980.

Osterink, Carole. "Gossips of Rivertown: News and Commentary About the City of Hudson, NY." https://gossipsofrivertown.blogspot.com.

Pratt, Sam. "The Bullet We Dodged: How the Cement War Was Won." *Our Town*, Winter 2010, 34–40.

Prezorski, Mark, and Jane Smith, eds. *Follies, Function & Form: Imagining Olana's Summer House*. Hudson, NY: Olana Partnership, 2016.

Ruttenber, E. M. *Footprints of the Red Men: Indian Geographical Names in the Valley of Hudson's River, the Valley of the Mohawk, and on the Delaware: Their Location and the Probable Meaning of Some of Them*. New York: New York State Historical Association, 1906.

Ryan, James Anthony. *Frederic Church's Olana: Architecture and Landscape as Art*. Hensonville, NY: Black Dome Press, 2001.

Sawyer, Sean E. "Partners in Design: Frederic Church and Calvert Vaux at Olana." *Hudson River Valley Review* 39, no. 1 (Autumn 2022): 60–72.

Schram, Margaret B. *Hudson's Merchants and Whalers: The Rise and Fall of a River Port 1783–1850*. Hensonville, NY: Black Dome Press, 2004.

Schuyler, David. *Embattled River: The Hudson and Modern Environmentalism*. Ithaca, NY: Cornell University Press, 2018.

———. *Sanctified Landscape: Writers, Artists, and the Hudson River Valley, 1820–1909*. Ithaca, NY: Cornell University Press, 2012.

———. "Saving Olana." *Hudson River Valley Review* 32, no. 2 (Spring 2016): 2–26.

Seamon, David. *Presenting Sense of Place to the Public: Background Planning for an Introductory Multi-Media Exhibit for American Landscape Paper Frederic Church's Olana*. Washington, DC: National Endowment for the Arts, 1992.

Shorto, Russell. *The Island at the Center of the World: The Epic Story of Dutch Manhattan and the Forgotten Colony That Shaped America*. New York: Vintage Books, 2005.

Siegel, Nancy. *Remember the Ladies: Women of the Hudson River School*. Catskill, NY: Thomas Cole National Historic Site, 2010.

———. *Susie M. Barstow: Redefining the Hudson River School*. London: Lund Humphries, 2023.

Siegel, Nancy, Kate Menconceri, and Amanda Malmstrom. *Women Reframe American Landscape: Susie Barstow & Her Circle, Contemporary Practices*. Catskill, NY: Thomas Cole National Historic Site, 2023.

Starr, Frederick S. *Bamboula! The Life and Times of Louis Moreau Gottschalk*. New York: Oxford University Press, 1995.

Stevens, Scott Manning. *Native Prospects: Indigeneity and Landscape*. Catskill, NY: Thomas Cole National Historic Site, 2024.

Swett, Benjamin. *The Hudson Valley: A Cultural Guide*. New York: Quantuck Lane Press, 2009.

Titus, Robert, and Johanna Titus. *The Hudson River Schools of Art and Their Ice Age Origins*. Bovina, NY: Purple Mountain Press, 2024.

———. "The Abyss," *Kaatskill Life: A Regional Journal* 17, no. 2 (Summer 2002): 56–63.

Toole, Robert M. *Historic Landscape Report: Olana State Historic Site*. Albany: New York State Office of Parks, Recreation and Historic Preservation, 1996.

———. *Landscape Gardens on the Hudson: A History*. Hensonville, NY: Black Dome Press, 2010.

Trager, James. *The New York Chronology: The Ultimate Compendium of Events, People, and Anecdotes from the Dutch to the Present*. New York: Harper Resource, 2003.

Trebilcock, Evelyn D., and Valerie Balint. *Glories of the Hudson: Frederic Edwin Church's Views from Olana*. Hudson, NY: Olana Partnership, 2009.

Vaux, Calvert. *Villas and Cottages: A Series of Designs*. New York: Harper and Brothers, 1864.

Wilmerding, John. *American Views: Essays on American Art*. Princeton, NJ: Princeton University Press, 1991.

———. *Master, Mentor, Master: Thomas Cole & Frederic Church*. Catskill, NY: Thomas Cole Historic Site, 2021.

Wulf, Andrea. *The Invention of Nature: Alexander von Humboldt's New World*. New York: Knopf, 2015.

Zabriskie, F. N. "'Old Colony' Papers: An Artist's Castle and Our Ride Thereto." *The Christian Intelligencer*, September 10, 1884.

Zukowski, Karen, and Julia B. Rosenbaum, eds. *Frederic Church's Olana on the Hudson: Art, Landscape, Architecture*. New York: Rizzoli Electa, 2018.

INDEX

ABOUT THE AUTHOR

ANNIK LAFARGE is a writer, editor, photographer, and lecturer. Her award-winning book *On the High Line: The Definitive Guide* was published in a third edition in 2024. Her comprehensive blog *LivinTheHighLine.com,* which she began in 2008, was selected by the Columbia University Libraries Web Resources Collection Program for inclusion in the Avery Library Historic Preservation and Urban Planning web archive, which ensures its continuing availability to researchers.

LaFarge is also the author of *Chasing Chopin,* a *New York Times Book Review* "Editors' Choice" that was longlisted for the PEN America Award for Biography and shortlisted for the William Saroyan International Prize. She has written for numerous publications including the *New York Times, Huff Post, Bark* magazine, the Library of Congress website, and *Publishers Weekly.* Her photography has been widely published in print and online publications and been licensed for commercial use. Since 2015 she has served as a trustee of the Waterfront Museum in Red Hook, Brooklyn, most recently as Chair.

SELECT TITLES FROM EMPIRE STATE EDITIONS

Salvatore Basile, *Fifth Avenue Famous: The Extraordinary Story of Music at St. Patrick's Cathedral.* Foreword by Most Reverend Timothy M. Dolan, Archbishop of New York

Daniel Campo, *The Accidental Playground: Brooklyn Waterfront Narratives of the Undesigned and Unplanned*

John Waldman, *Heartbeats in the Muck: The History, Sea Life, and Environment of New York Harbor, Revised Edition*

John Waldman (ed.), *Still the Same Hawk: Reflections on Nature and New York*

Joseph B. Raskin, *The Routes Not Taken: A Trip Through New York City's Unbuilt Subway System*

North Brother Island: The Last Unknown Place in New York City. Photographs by Christopher Payne, A History by Randall Mason, Essay by Robert Sullivan

Stephen Miller, *Walking New York: Reflections of American Writers from Walt Whitman to Teju Cole*

Joanne Witty and Henrik Krogius, *Brooklyn Bridge Park: A Dying Waterfront Transformed*

Sharon Egretta Sutton, *When Ivory Towers Were Black: A Story about Race in America's Cities and Universities*

Pamela Hanlon, *A Wordly Affair: New York, the United Nations, and the Story Behind Their Unlikely Bond*

David J. Goodwin, *Left Bank of the Hudson: Jersey City and the Artists of 111 1st Street.* Foreword by DW Gibson

Nandini Bagchee, *Counter Institution: Activist Estates of the Lower East Side*

Elizabeth Macaulay-Lewis and Matthew M. McGowan (eds.), *Classical New York: Discovering Greece and Rome in Gotham*

Susan Opotow and Zachary Baron Shemtob (eds.), *New York after 9/11*

Andrew Feffer, *Bad Faith: Teachers, Liberalism, and the Origins of McCarthyism*

Colin Davey with Thomas A. Lesser, *The American Museum of Natural History and How It Got That Way.* Forewords by Neil deGrasse Tyson and Kermit Roosevelt III

Wendy Jean Katz, *Humbug: The Politics of Art Criticism in New York City's Penny Press*

Lolita Buckner Inniss, *The Princeton Fugitive Slave: The Trials of James Collins Johnson*

Mike Jaccarino, *America's Last Great Newspaper War: The Death of Print in a Two-Tabloid Town*

Angel Garcia, *The Kingdom Began in Puerto Rico: Neil Connolly's Priesthood in the South Bronx*

Jim Mackin, *Notable New Yorkers of Manhattan's Upper West Side: Bloomingdale–Morningside Heights*

Matthew Spady, *The Neighborhood Manhattan Forgot: Audubon Park and the Families Who Shaped It*

Robert O. Binnewies, *Palisades: 100,000 Acres in 100 Years*

Marilyn S. Greenwald and Yun Li, *Eunice Hunton Carter: A Lifelong Fight for Social Justice*

Jeffrey A. Kroessler, *Sunnyside Gardens: Planning and Preservation in a Historic Garden Suburb*
Elizabeth Macaulay-Lewis, *Antiquity in Gotham: The Ancient Architecture of New York City*
Ron Howell, *King Al: How Sharpton Took the Throne*
Jean Arrington with Cynthia S. LaValle, *From Factories to Palaces: Architect Charles B. J. Snyder and the New York City Public Schools*. Foreword by Peg Breen
Boukary Sawadogo, *Africans in Harlem: An Untold New York Story*
Alvin Eng, *Our Laundry, Our Town: My Chinese American Life from Flushing to the Downtown Stage and Beyond*
Stephanie Azzarone, *Heaven on the Hudson: Mansions, Monuments, and Marvels of Riverside Park*
Ron Goldberg, *Boy with the Bullhorn: A Memoir and History of ACT UP New York*. Foreword by Dan Barry
Peter Quinn, *Cross Bronx: A Writing Life*
Mark Bulik, *Ambush at Central Park: When the IRA Came to New York*
Matt Dallos, *In the Adirondacks: Dispatches from the Largest Park in the Lower 48*
Brandon Dean Lamson, *Caged: A Teacher's Journey Through Rikers, or How I Beheaded the Minotaur*
Raj Tawney, *Colorful Palate: Savored Stories from a Mixed Life*
Edward Cahill, *Disorderly Men*
Joseph Heathcott, *Global Queens: An Urban Mosaic*
Francis R. Kowsky with Lucille Gordon, *Hell on Color, Sweet on Song: Jacob Wrey Mould and the Artful Beauty of Central Park*
Jill Jonnes, *South Bronx Rising: The Rise, Fall, and Resurrection of an American City, Third Edition*
Barbara G. Mensch, *A Falling-Off Place: The Transformation of Lower Manhattan*
David J. Goodwin, *Midnight Rambles: H. P. Lovecraft in Gotham*
Felipe Luciano, *Flesh and Spirit: Confessions of a Young Lord*
Maximo G. Martinez, *Sojourners in the Capital of the World: Garifuna Immigrants*
Jennifer Baum, *Just City: Growing Up on the Upper West Side When Housing Was a Human Right*
Davida Siwisa James, *Hamilton Heights and Sugar Hill: Alexander Hamilton's Old Harlem Neighborhood Through the Centuries*
Annik LaFarge, *On the High Line: The Definitive Guide, Third Edition*. Foreword by Rick Dark
Marie Carter, *Mortimer and the Witches: A History of Nineteenth-Century Fortune Tellers*
Alice Sparberg Alexiou, *Devil's Mile: The Rich, Gritty History of the Bowery*. Foreword by Peter Quinn
Carey Kasten and Brenna Moore, *Mutuality in El Barrio: Stories of the Little Sisters of the Assumption Family Health Service*. Foreword by Norma Benítez Sánchez
Kimberly A. Orcutt, *The American Art-Union: Utopia and Skepticism in the Antebellum Era*
Jonathan Butler, *Join the Conspiracy: How a Brooklyn Eccentric Got Lost on the Right, Infiltrated the Left, and Brought Down the Biggest Bombing Network in New York*
Nicole Gelinas, *Movement: New York's Long War to Take Back Its Streets from the Car*
Jack Hodgson, *Young Reds in the Big Apple: The New York Young Pioneers of America, 1923–1934*

Lynn Ellsworth, *Wonder City: How to Reclaim Human-Scale Urban Life*
Walter Zev Feldman, *From the Bronx to the Bosphorus: Klezmer and Other Displaced Musics of New York*
Larry Racioppo, *Here Down on Dark Earth: Loss and Remembrance in New York City*
Bonnie Yochelson, *Too Good to Get Married: The Life and Photographs of Miss Alice Austen*
David Brown Morris, *Ten Thousand Central Parks: A Climate-Change Parable*
Eve M. Kahn, *Queen of Bohemia Predicts Own Death: The Forgotten Journalist Zoe Anderson Norris, 1860-1914*
Miriam Chaiken, *Creative Ozone: The Artists of Westbeth*
Stefanie Mercado Altman, Claire Altman, and Stan Altman, *Twice Blessed: A Story of Unconditional Love*. Foreword by Stephen G. Post
Stephanie Azzarone, *Fabulous Fountains of New York*
Larry Racioppo, *Memorial '76*. Foreword by Kevin Baker
Phyllis Ross, *Stories in Fabric: The Design Works of Bedford Stuyvesant*. Foreword by Judith Jones
Paul Schmitz, *New York's Family Grocer: The Story of D'Agostino Supermarkets*

For a complete list, visit www.fordhampress.com/empire-state-editions.